Praise for *CHOICES*

"For me, it is always a tremendous added blessing to know the author personally. In this case and with Ron James, he is the real deal! His story is thought-provoking, challenges my heart and his story is a real page turner; as I am always wondering 'what's next' and 'what if'. I can hardly wait to buy my first 10 copies and give them as gifts to my best friends and see how this book can change their lives and the CHOICES they make."

John M. Langel Sr. – co-worker and friend

"Ron James has written a book that has a message for every person -- whether they are in a physical prison or a self-made prison. Ron's book, *Choices,* helps the reader learn from the life experience of one who took the wrong turn and then discovered the right path. I have been deeply touched by Ron's humility and deep desire to break free from old habits and turn his life around. His commitment to attesting to the power of Jesus Christ to transform his life is a sermon in itself. I hope that Ron's book, *Choices,* is shared in every prison in America and that every prisoner of the soul finds in it the fresh air of liberation."

Dilip R. Abayasekara, Ph.D.
Author of The Path of the Genie
Toastmasters International President, 2005-2006
CEO, Dr. Dilip, LLC

"Ron James is a man who knows what he is talking about. CHOICES will humble you, inspire you, and make a positive difference in your life!"

Tracey C. Jones, best-!

D1114076

"What you first discover about Ron James, rather through personal encounter or through his writings, is an incredibly charismatic personality who is fully in love with life. Ron's book, *Choices*, is an incredible journey from the depths of despair and hopelessness to the exhilarating heights of a life fully lived. *Choices* is a compelling personal story that cannot be ignored - an inspiring message of hope and triumph. Ron's message is touching hearts and changing lives! Readers of his book will be personally stirred, as I have been, by the transformative power of Ron James' message. Through *Choices* you will gain an increased appreciation for the freedoms we enjoy and a renewed zest for life!"

Russell G. Kulp, Ed.M.
Associate Dean, Central Penn College
School of Business and Communications

WENDY

Lessons Learned from a Repeat Offender

CHOICES

Ronald L. James

iUniverse LLC
Bloomington

PROV 3:5-6

CHOICES
LESSONS LEARNED FROM A REPEAT OFFENDER

iUniverse books may be ordered through booksellers or by contacting:

iUniverse
1663 Liberty Drive
Bloomington, IN 47403
www.iuniverse.com
1-800-Authors (1-800-288-4677)

ISBN: 978-1-4917-1991-6 (sc)
ISBN: 978-1-4917-1992-3 (e)

Printed in the United States of America.

iUniverse rev. date: 01/30/2014

INTRODUCTION

THIS PROGRESSIVELY EXPRESSIVE AUTOBIOGRAPHY is not an instructional, self-help book to keep one out of jail, nor is it about crime, addiction, abuse, religion, conspiracy theories, or about getting rich. Rather, it is a question of urgency and importance - DO YOU WANT TO GO TO JAIL TODAY?

The reader is presented with vivid images of the author's experiences, personal battles, CHOICES, and the consequences and tragic results of those choices.

The typical reader may pick up this book with the intent of judging the author's lifestyle, with the comparing assurance that what happened to the author would never happen to them.

What they will find are the harsh realities in the similarities that mirror their own lives and, if not addressed, could lead them down the same path. Some names have been changed to protect those still living; however, most named in this book have unfortunately succumbed to those harsh realities of living life on the street, chasing the dream of better living through modern chemistry …so to speak.

If others learn from our mistakes and it saves them from the pain that we ourselves experienced, then it was not all in vain.

Our Daily Bread, March 15, 2012

TO THE AUTHOR'S CREDIT:

- The author has had notable life experiences as an authority on the subject of incarceration within the prison system. His experiences of 25-plus years – having served in four state prisons, ten county jails, one state hospital and five rehab facilities in three states – spanned the years 1984 to 2012 and provides the author with tremendous insight into prison life.

- The goal of this literary encounter is to allow the reader to identify with the author's experiences and lifestyle. Whether good or bad in the eyes of the reader, these choices caused him to pay the ultimate price with his life and time. The hope is that this book keeps people free, exceeds all expectations for everyone who reads it, and that they will be touched, affected and forever changed by the events in the life of the author... and hopefully, will be impacted in such a way that they consider their own choices and not encounter the same undesirable consequences.

- Unique and revelatory, this book is detailed, emotional, funny, heartfelt, and thought-provoking. In your reading, be open-minded about the purpose of making good life choices by being informed, equipped, uplifted and empowered by the lessons shared.

- Thank you and may God bless all who read this and share the lessons learned.

DEDICATION

THIS BOOK IS DEDICATED TO MY MOTHER

To Miriam Louise Eberhart James (5/31/36 – 12/19/04), better known to all as "MiMi". It is the gift of heavenly love you possessed that allowed you to endure the hardship, pain, and suffering I so undeservingly gave you. You watched me destroy myself with pure selfishness, yet you loved me through it all.

I thank God for my fond memories of you. It was your kindness and love that passed from your heart into mine, which now allows me to share this book with the world. I will forever love you.

ACKNOWLEDGEMENTS AND SPECIAL THANKS

FIRST OF ALL, TO the friends and family who believed in me and saw something good in me through all my mess, this book is a reflection of their hope during my 25-plus year journey.

To my mentor, teacher and friend, Robert L. Jolles... whose persuasive skills motivated and influenced me to write this book. He began with three simple words..."Writing is writing"...and encouraged me to take it from there and, for that, I will be forever grateful. This book is dedicated to you and your special friendship. See you in the pit. In addition, very special thanks go out to Wanda Clayton for her talents in typing my manuscript.

My brother-in-Law, George A. Rucker (Coach)...who allowed me the opportunity to fill his brother's shoes in his absence and, without question, knew this day would come. You will always be Coach to me, and many thanks to you.

To my siblings, John, Lori, Marsan, and Susan...whom I thank for their support and never refused to give up on me. Lori, my heart goes out to you for positioning yourself on my behalf no matter what the circumstances were; I am eternally grateful.

My DIVA, Ottamissiah (Missy) Moore...many friendships have been had over the years, but none have come close to the unconditional harmony we share. You saw this story well before it was written because (no surprise) that is what you do. To my friends Thomas Armstrong, David Artist, Thelma V. Brosko, Lisa Bankert-Buck, Chaplain Drew Degier, John Hill, Larry Neff, Amanda Hipple, my spiritual brothers John Langel, Steve Sands & Keith Sultzbaugh, and to Elliott Pinkcus...all of whom have helped me to realize my gifts and talents as a leader. Your continued friendship, prayers and belief in my abilities will empower me to reach consistently for higher levels.

To my daughter, Lanaya James...who endured growing up without me through her young years. You have given me the hope to be the best dad a daughter would ever have in this season and those to come.

And finally, to my future wife and family...if the information revealed does not drive you away, then I look forward to sharing, giving and fulfilling all your needs...selflessly...for our lifetime.

P.S. My future wife...I did meet her and we were married September 21, 2013, even AFTER she read the book!

FOREWORD

Robert L. Jolles

CHOICES. WHAT A SIMPLE, and appropriate, title for this book. Comedian Buddy Hackett once said this: "As a child, my family's menu consisted of two choices: take it or leave it." Choice sounds so easy, but the truth in making the right choice is anything but easy.

Ron James is my friend. I made this choice years ago. I made that choice without ever speaking to him, seeing him, or knowing much about him. I made that choice by reading a letter he sent to me from prison.

When Ron's letter arrived at my desk, right off the bat, it caught my attention. Although I can receive over one hundred emails a day, I had not received a hand written letter in years. Ron made the choice to write it, and I made the choice to read it...carefully.

That letter, and the many letters that followed, changed the fate of not one, but two people. The more letters I read from Ron, the more I felt there was a deeper story that needed told by Ron.

In my life, I have mentored many people who have hopes and dreams of writing a book. At some point, you have to move past the dream of writing a book and make it a reality. You have to get your hands on a computer keyboard and do it.

In one of my letters to Ron, I threw out the idea of actually writing his own book. I sent him this quote to help him on his way:

Planning to write is not writing.
Thinking about writing is not writing.
Talking about writing is not writing.
Researching and outlining to write is not writing.
None of this is writing.
Writing is writing.

Most choose not to follow through, but Ron made a different choice. He chose to put that poem up on his wall, stay true to his dream, tell his story, and write his book. He did not have the luxury of sitting in front of a computer, setting up files, and manipulating the text as he went along. Ron James was given paper and a pen, and he began to write… oh, did this man write! Ten pages grew to fifty, and then to one hundred pages. He surpassed five hundred, and then one thousand pages.

Finally, I received a letter from Ron telling me he had finished the first draft of his book. Apparently, he went through plenty of pens, used up a whole lot of paper, and missed out on a lot of 'yard time' by sitting in his cell writing because his first draft was exactly 1,825 pages long.

When I begrudgingly informed Ron that he would have to shorten this a bit, he made another choice. He chose to keep working, and he edited that handwritten manuscript.

For most who write, editing means copying and pasting, moving text around here and there on a computer screen, and inputting bits and pieces as needed. However, for Ron, it meant studying what he had written, and writing it *again*. Carefully working through his existing manuscript, he rewrote it. Then he rewrote it again, and finally, he trimmed it down to a mere 538 pages. I should know; he mailed it to me, and when I need to be inspired, I look at it. I do not just think about the text in hand; I think about the over 3,000 pages of self-discovery to get to this point.

Clearly, Ron James made a choice to grind, work, and not give up because he had a story he wanted you to hear. In fact, he has created a powerful description of the decades of life choices he has made: Some good and some not so good, and the consequences that came with those choices. He lived those choices and throughout his twenty years of incarceration, he had a front row seat that allowed him to view the impact of these choices. His sincere passion is to help others by teaching you what he has learned.

In searching for the meaning in the choices he has made, he has evolved from a man of thought to a man of action. In searching for the meaning in his life, he made a choice to become a man of faith and to work hard to be a better man each and every day. In searching for a way to help others, he made the choice to chronicle these choices. He did not do this because he wanted to unburden his soul; he did it because he wanted to help others learn from these choices.

This is a story about a man who has chosen a new path. It is a path of redemption and it is a path of self-disclosure. He has chosen this path because his ultimate desire is not just to tell you what he has done, or what he intends to do. He has chosen this path because, through these pages, he has a sincere desire to reach out and help you with your choices.

I have always believed that wisdom consists of three things: success, failure, and a conscious knowledge of the lessons learned from each. If throughout your life, you have only known success, I consider you a fortunate person, but not necessarily a wise person. If throughout your life, you have only known failure, I would consider you a less fortunate person, but not necessarily a wise person. However, if you have experienced both success and failure, and you can articulate what you have learned, I would consider you a wise person.

Ron James is a very wise person and he became a wise person the only way he knew how: he earned it. Not by living a life of success and failure, but by documenting, scrutinizing and learning from the life he has lived.

Poet George Herbert once wrote: "The shortest answer is doing." The journey you are about to take, as you read through the words of Ron James, reflects that very sentiment.

In a prison cell, with pen and paper in hand, Ron went beyond the dream of just writing a book and helping others to learn about better choices. He acted on this dream and now, through his words and his wisdom, he extends his hand and offers to help you with the choices you might make. Grasp that hand and listen to his words. They come from a man, a very wise man, who knows about choices.

CONTENTS

PREFACE

I HAVE HEARD IT said that insanity is doing the same thing over and over and expecting different results. I beg to differ. This statement sounds profound coming from those who claim their own sanity. My take on insanity is doing the same thing over and over and expecting just what would happen, assuming the outcome and doing it anyway. Crazy, right? I am not so sure.

If you take a look at some of the greatest men and women who ever walked the earth, such as Mother Teresa, Thurgood Marshall, Albert Einstein, George Washington Carver and Steve Jobs, just to name a few, they were considered brilliant people – geniuses in their own right. They had an inner desire to press forward despite hatred, failures, challenges, opposition and conventional wisdom, even to despite sanity. Something on the inside drove them to keep going and not give up. I share that inner drive with those in greatness, which is the fine line between insanity and my own genius.

Frankly speaking, I have allowed myself over the years to become the research monkey or a crash-test dummy to an insanely selfish lifestyle that would have otherwise left me for dead. As you read the consequences of my actions throughout this book, you will begin to understand that I have done enough time in prison facilities to pass the test and become that certified monkey or dummy.

CHOICES is not merely a title, but evidence of living fact. I have spent 25-plus years of my life incarcerated…meaning I was confined to, walked around in, ate, slept and woke up in jails, prisons or correctional facilities of some form every single day for a cumulated period of 25 years!

There was no run to the distributor for a case of beer with the guys, no trip to the grocery store when you were hungry, no pizza delivery on game day, no night out with your friends watching the latest R-rated movie, no hang-time after school, no extracurricular activities, and certainly no cell phones to be had!

My experiences will be shared to help readers, young and old alike, people of all ethnicities and creeds, first-time offenders, hardened men and women, and those who may never see the light of day to not make the same mistakes I made…or at least to make better choices once they are released.

Regardless of your situation, your next move can be your best move – you need to trust God in all aspects of your life and you will experience a life greater than you ever imagined.

This book will start with a question and ironically end with the same question. You will be the deciding factor in the answer. So ask yourself, "Do YOU want to go to jail today?"

If your answer was yes, at least you are secure in the fact that if you continue doing what you are currently doing, or hanging with friends who tell you it is okay and that you will not get caught, you will likely end up in a not so familiar place, sitting inside a cold, 9' x 9' concrete cement or cinder block cell – or hole, for those already incarcerated – with a steel sink and toilet that will be shared with your 'cellie' from who knows what part of the country, and left to your own devices.

If your answer to the question was no, you are more likely being truthful. My statement to you then is that if any of your actions or lifestyle reflects any part of breaking the law, the possibility exists that you could end up in jail…unless you change your actions and lifestyle.

My suggestion to you is begin now with making better choices because all actions produce consequences, whether good or bad, and it is my hope for all you reading that your life will be filled with good consequences.

Insanity, for the purpose of this book, is going to jail when you do not have to. I want to save you the time; I am begging you to not do the crime. Life is so much more enjoyable without the burden of incarceration.

BETTER

POEM BY: MIRIAM 'MIMI' JAMES

Good better best,
may you never rest
Until the good gets better,
and the better best

"We are born with an innate value that sometimes can never be diminished by anyone else; value yourself enough to act in your own best interest."

-Mary Steffy

"Planning to write is not writing. Thinking about writing is not writing. Talking about writing is not writing. Researching and outlining to write is not writing. None of this is writing; writing is writing".

-Robert L. Jolles

CHOICE ONE
DREAM

A GREAT NUMBER OF events transpired before I actually put the ink to paper and decided to write this book. None was as revealing as the opening statement you have just read. 'Writing is writing' are the three words that came alive only after I chose to put them into action and then onto paper. Call it divine development if you will. In order for me to reach this stage in my life and process each event the way I have, a number of things had to occur: first, I had to examine my entire life and its years of false beliefs. I had to get rid of what did not work and replace it with new information that created a new mind-set in the way I now do things. In other words, think new and act new.

How I perceive and receive information now dictates the outcome of events I create for myself. The external things that influenced me were my mother, father, family and friends, the neighborhood where I grew up, the schools I attended and that all-important first kiss, but they all left me with the question of what was next.

Furthermore, the internal things that I had difficulty processing, things like feelings, rejection or shame and abandonment, along with those external factors have played a major role in my development. These factors have amounted to who I have become…the Ronald Lloyd James of today.

Whether we like it or not, accept it or not, it would seem each event in our lives have the potential to wire us into who we will become. My question to you is "Will your encounter with this book change your life?" As you read on, time will tell.

In the world of criminal justice, there is a thing called Forensic Science, which helps investigators solve crimes. It is said by the experts that it is scientifically impossible for two human beings to come in contact with each other and not be affected by one another. I believe this to be true, but even more so in the spiritual realm. Somehow each event, whether by reason or complex situations, affects us in one form or another. Everything seems to matter, from the most trivial encounter to the most profound experience. Everything matters, and my birth ranks somewhere in between.

Born June 16th, 1962, I was a breast-fed child and after my feeding, I was placed in a crib, bassinette or sometimes rocked to sleep in someone's arms. This was common in order for mom to have a break or to have time to do motherly things.

Most of the time, my sleep was short lived since I was an active baby in both mind and body, and often I would lay awake and cry…so much so that my mom would continue to breast feed me. Cry-feed, cry-feed, cry-feed was the repeated cycle more often than not because I wanted her affection until I would finally pass out and sleep.

I wanted to be picked up and held every time I cried, and it was resolved by feeding. Mom determined I was just greedy so she stopped breast-feeding and placed me on the bottle.

How could anyone know my real need for affection was being met with a substance…milk…and that it was something I could never get enough of? This event was so deeply rooted that it has taken me a lifetime to uncover and deal with my real issues.

It all began at 59th and Lansdowne Avenue in West Philly. A duplex called home with a family already in existence. My big brother, John, was named after my dad and was five years my senior, and he was my idol. About 20 months after my arrival, my sister Lori was born. She was my angel, and fondly named Bibba…"Houston, we have a problem!"…Now my mother had to deal with two babies, feeding became territorial, and we had to try to come to an understanding.

For the past 20 months, it was all about Ron James. Every bottle under that roof was meant for one person, ME! It was bad enough that my mom took me off the breast and called me greedy, now I had to share time and milk with a stranger. Give her the breast and I will take the bottles.

One day while Bibba was feeding, I found myself committing my first offense. I was less than 2 years old, and I was breaking and entering my sister's crib because I figured out that she had something I wanted; I was on a mission to get it. I went into action with her bottle in my sights and proceeded to move up and into her crib.

Within seconds, I had the prized possession in my mouth when all of a sudden my sister began to cry. I had to find a way to cover my tracks and pacify the victim, so I grabbed the closest thing I could get my hands on and that was a feather. I stuck it into her mouth and it silenced her. Quick thinking on my part, or so I thought, but this single act of pleasing my own desires nearly killed my sister. It was not long before she started to gag, choke and gasp for air. The alarm sounded when she started crying and my mom came to the rescue.

The next 'all about me' encounter was Easter Sunday 1964. My mom had decked me out in a yellow and beige knicker suit with a matching hat. We were all on our way to church that morning when she was distracted by something that needed her immediate attention.

So there I was, left on the couch in the front room, all dressed up with no place to go. I decided to take a little walk. I grabbed my high chair and pushed it up against the front door. I climbed up, unlocked the door, turned the dead bolt lock and unfastened the chain. Not quite two years old and I was free! Free at last!

I made it outside and down the street. My freedom, however, was short lived as I was soon discovered by one of our neighbors, who spotted me playing in the alley next to her house. The neighbor immediately called my mom on the phone to alert her.

I had found a can of oil based paint, opened it and then began to add black designs to my suit. As my mom approached, I knew something was wrong when she began to cry out, "Oh no!" When she showed up, I greeted her with a big smile. As I stood in my yellow and beige knicker suit with my newly painted designs, mom was not angry, she was grateful that I was ok and nothing worse had happened, like walking out into traffic and getting hit by a car.

Years later, I watched her praise God with joy as she shared this story with me and her tearful smile said it all. My mom never said I was bad; my actions were only explained as mischievous or naughty.

Call it whatever you want, no matter what I did, I always got some kind of attention. Attention was all I ever desired and I learned at an early age how to read my mom's body language in order to get the most of her attention. I was in tune to her every move and all of her facial expressions. When I did something wrong, she was loving and always quick with discipline. When I did something right, there was no stopping the attention she would give and I loved it!

One day I was with mom at one of the neighborhood stores on Lansdowne Avenue. I was four years old and smart enough to know that stuffing a bunch of red gummy fish into my mouth and pockets without asking was wrong!

My mother's looks could cut you like a knife. Her discipline would begin with the 'death stare'…you all know the one I am talking about. First, she would lock both eyes on her target (in most cases it was me), then oh so slowly and with precision, her eyes would make a connection that would register directly into your soul. Second, her right eye would slightly close to a squint and this stare was very subtle and distinct. Finally, if you somehow missed it and did not understand, then her left eye would slightly open and would peer at you. At this point, you knew you were in for it!

Now all of this was done within a few seconds, meaning… for your eyes only. Most of the time I would get the message and straighten up; however, this day I was too far gone. I was so caught up in enjoying the flavor of my gummy fishes that her next move was a swift crack to my backside; it was then I knew something was wrong. She explained to me in front of the owner it was wrong to steal. I said I understood, but somehow I missed the life message from the whole encounter.

Around this same time, I had my first experience with alcohol. One day after my parents entertained friends and family, my mother discovered I had cigarette ashes all over my mouth. I was helping to clean up by finishing the leftover beers that were still on the coffee table. Little did I know that those bottles had become ashtrays for our guests to extinguish their cigarettes. My mom was not mad because I was innocent in my actions, and I was satisfied after receiving her attention and affection. She let me pass out in her arms to sleep it off.

My dad's name was Johnny Boy, known as the king of the castle who was an aggressive entrepreneur / hustler from North Philly. He did not complete the sixth grade, but you would never have known this when having a conversation with him. My dad's gift of gab could give President Barack Obama a run for his money.

His empire was founded on good old American hard work. By the age of 21, he acquired his first garage, his business grew and he eventually became the owner of two gas service stations in the city. He purchased our home on Wanamaker Street with a half block of rental storage spaces and parking garages with an auto shop.

Our home was a beautiful two story white stucco-faced building, commonly known as 'The White House'. I went to a private school called Christ Memorial Parrish located in West Philadelphia, which was a multicultural school with an ethnic mix of Asian, Black, Hispanic and White children. Some kids had problems adjusting to coming to school. Some cried for their parents and wanted to go home and some would piss in their pants because they forgot to tell the teacher they had to go to the bathroom.

However, like most of my peers, I had a normal everyday school life. There was visual learning, naptime, lunch, and games. I was well adjusted for the most part. We had a class bully, but I did not mind fighting or throwing my weight around. There was a rule that was hammered in my head from both of my parents and that was, "Ronnie, you are not to fight!"

One day when that classroom bully decided to put his hands on me by punching me repeatedly in the chest, I was restrained only by the words of my parents, which echoed in my soul while his actions upon me took place. When I got home, I told my mom about the incident. She sat me down and began to explain that she did not want me to get into trouble by starting fights...BUT if I got into something because of someone else, it was okay for me to defend myself.

Oh boy did that change the rules or what! From that point on, I tried to justify my actions while manipulating others into believing I was a victim, but I never really was. I caused most of the situations I got myself into and I only confessed to things when I was in a corner.

Each day a small van would pick me up at our front door and cart me off to school. It was during one of these trips that I had my first encounter with self. I heard a small, very subtle and clear voice speak, "Ron, why are you here?" I was not sure and had no idea how to answer that question. As the van kept moving, I looked out of the window and noticed life seemed to take on a different meaning at that point, and I realized there was something special about me. Feeling as though I was born to do great things, life suddenly became bigger than who I was. Things and people mattered, yet I wondered what life was all about, and what did I have to do with it?

As I got older, I began to notice my mother was no longer concerned whether or not I confessed to any wrong doing. She became judge and jury while taking up alliances with household objects to discipline me.

Now, you need to understand that I grew up in the sixties era, meaning if you were disrespectful or did anything wrong, your neighbors could discipline you. Then you were brought home to your mother, who would most likely have her way with you...followed by your father, who would come home from a long day of work, leaving you to deal with the brunt of his frustrations.

In today's era, my mother would be sitting upstate with a number, instead of her name, for beatings she administered. "WHY?" you may ask…because she would grab anything that was within reach and bring fire to my butt, including wooden spoons, spatulas or a rolled up newspaper or magazine.

Ah yes! Let us not forget the most feared household object known to all children of the sixties as the undisputed champion…Survey says…THE EXTENSION CORD! Woo wee, you bet your sweet bottom, if you EVVVVVER lived through one of those events, you would come out of it with all kinds of welts and battle scars to prove it! I learned quickly to respect the extension cord and the fury of the person who controlled it, and, as usual, I found out the hard way.

Mom caught me doing something out of order, the verdict was always "Guilty". Before I was sentenced and punished by the extension cord, I did everything in my power to get out of harm's way. I held on to that cord for dear life! I ran, screamed, cried, lied and pleaded for her to reconsider, but NOTHING mattered. My mother went into combat mode with the events starting out like a scene from the movie *The Matrix*. My body had moves, but unlike slow motion, I could not keep up and mom was in the zone and was having her way.

I was able to catch a break and I screamed out "Mom, you hit my skeeter"! (private parts) and she stopped. It worked… my lie worked…or so I thought! As I clutched the part between my legs she supposedly hit, she said in her sweet voice, "Move your hands so I can see". She did not buy into my game nor did the discipline end there. This pause only gave her a second wind, and when she got it, she commenced to swinging again. After a few more swings, she stopped. Those beatings only last a few minutes, but they seemed like an eternity!

Mom always insisted I should be polite and instructed me to exercise good behavior in front of others. When someone spoke to me, I should always speak back. I was taught to say "No sir, yes sir" or "No ma'am, yes ma'am". I was taught how to open doors for people, especially for the elderly and women, put away groceries, empty the trash, clean up after myself and help my mom with my three younger sisters - Lori, Marsan, and Susan. I enjoyed doing these things and did them well, always with a smile. As a result, I was rewarded with praise or sometimes small gifts.

On the other hand, and unlike my mother, the men of the family were "go getters". They had no problem chasing a dollar. Most of the men in our family were associated with some type of crime, from major drug distribution to running numbers and everything in between. Call it a plethora of criminals if you will. There were street gang members, stick up men, bank robbers, flim flam artist, drug addicts, dealers and gangsters. What a portfolio!

A major part of my life was formed by the spoken (and unspoken) belief system that was administered and displayed among my family. At what point did my family members readily accept criminal activity? I am not sure, but what I found interesting was the significant aspect of the issue. It had to do with the mindset of the men in the family who chased the dollar and the women, therein, who spent those dollars. The attitude of my family was "get the money first, and we will deal with whatever comes later".

Somewhere along the line, I developed a mindset to challenge the system and those in charge. Between the ages of six and eight, I began taking chances even if it brought pain or embarrassment…so much so, I was willing to go against "The Man".

I remember one particular day, I picked on a police officer to be the brunt of my jokes. He was driving down our street with his windows rolled down and I began to hit him with a barrage of words that started with the letters M, F, B, and P. A sailor may have appreciated my new lingo, but the officer certainly did not. He pulled his patrol car over and got out.

This large, clean cut, grandfather looking figure of an Irish man in uniform stood over me with badge and gun. His superiority, stature and authority were evident and the posture of his body and tone in his voice commanded respect. Until this time, I thought my mother was the only person on earth who possessed the "death stare", but I was wrong, and after a stern lecture he placed me in the back of his patrol car. The only thing that was racing through my mind was, "Please do not let my parents find out what just happened."

I went into my survival mode. Learning this type of thinking could be turned on and off at will, it developed into a powerful tool of manipulation and became part of my personality. I changed and became very cordial, adjusted my mannerism and answered all the officer's questions with a "Yes Sir, No Sir". After he was done, I apologized and it worked. A few minutes later, he opened the door and let me go.

Looking at things in hindsight, I wonder if my life events would have played out differently had this been my last time in the back of a police car. What was I doing? Did it really work? Who was I getting over on? Was the joke really on yours truly after all of these years?

No matter where I went, my troubles seem to follow me. One of the neighborhood boys and I were out playing in front of my grandparents house one afternoon. He and I began a game of name-calling and he decided to say something about my mother. I was overly protective of mom and, in those days, no one said anything about someone's mother unless they were ready to mix it up. All he did was associate my mom with an ant, YES an ant!

His timing could not have been worse. At that very moment my grandfather just happened to be driving down the street and in the front passenger seat, was my mom sitting with her southern smile. The only thing I was able to process in my mind was that this boy just said something I did not understand, but that infuriated me. It did not sit well with me and I felt challenged, so I went to work leaping on him with all fours; I had the home court advantage with mom and granddad as an audience. I performed quite well jacking him up, and as my now ex-friend entered into a daze, my mom jumped out of the car.

She took me into custody and dragged me to my grandparent's front porch. She demanded to know what the fight was all about and then asked, "Isn't he your friend?" When she paused to hear my response, I said "This guy called you a bitch!" Her reaction to what I said was more of a surprise then the lie I told on this guy. She said, "What? The next time kick his damn butt!" Mom spoke in a tone of voice that clearly meant business, and I was later applauded as a hero.

My mother was kind, warm and congenial, and affectionately known by everyone as Mimi. Her disposition was keen and sharp; she was entertaining and brilliant, her words tasteful and charming. However, she would cuss you out in a heartbeat if you ever took her kindness for weakness or messed with any of her five children, especially me.

Now that I was a hero and in mom's good graces, I felt I could do no wrong. I began to believe in my own lies more and less on the absolute truth, taking on the concept that it was ok to be deceitful in order to get out of tight situations …or anything for that matter.

Lying became automatic, naturally saying whatever came to mind. The troubling part is that my dishonesty became my normal way of thinking. This mindset placed me on a self-destructive crash course beginning with deception, thievery, and hiding items I did not want found.

I created a stash spot in my toy chest located in our family basement to hide my most valuable secrets. Deep within the wooden chest held one of my most prized possessions. I would wait until everyone was preoccupied then creep down to the basement to check on my stash. After I was able to reach the bench, I would lift the top open and pull out my toys one by one to uncover my prize.

It was as if I was digging for hidden treasure. When I removed the last toy from the chest, I noticed that my body began to change with anticipation and excitement causing a rush-like high to overtake me. My heart was beating fast and my ears ringing to the sound of my panting breath. As I lifted the booty to the surface, I became sexually stimulated. There it was, my eyes fixated on the forbidden fruit…a porn magazine I found while rummaging through someone's trash on our block!

No matter how many times I flipped through the pages, the pictures always provided something new. I enjoyed looking at the variety of beautiful women, and, as their images were being scorched deeply into my mind and soul, it seemed as though I could never get enough. There I sat, intensely viewing each part of their body, from the color of their hair down to their toe nail polish. When I had my fill, I placed the magazine back into my hiding place just as carefully as I took it out. I knew I would be in big trouble if my dad ever found this. Speaking of dad…

My dad owned a Sunoco Station on 54th and Parkside Avenue in West Philadelphia. He also owned an Exxon Station on Market Street in Wilmington, Delaware. His newest purchase was a Mobile service station on Route 309 in Montgomeryville, PA. He also owned the property on Wanamaker, a bar, two stores, the White House and the garages – and all of this is amazing for a man who never completed the 6th grade! He wanted to move closer to his newest establishment in Montgomeryville, so he bought a new four-bedroom house right in the middle of a new development built by Haggie Developers called Pennwood Gardens. I found moving to be very exciting with all of the packing, cleaning, boxing up the U-Haul truck.

My excitement came to a screeching halt when my dad discovered my hidden treasure. YES! The porn magazine had been discovered...Oh boy, was I in trouble now! I got a severe tongue lashing by both parents, knowing the only thing that saved me was the fact we were in the middle of moving. Had it been any other moment in time, I probably would not be here to tell the rest of this story!

My last memory of Philadelphia was one summer when I was walking down the street toward the White House, alone but not alone, and that ever present inner voice was clearly with me this day. The voice spoke and said "Look down". I looked down at the ground and I am wondering what it is I was supposed to be looking for. Nevertheless, I continued looking. I was standing on the sidewalk and began to examine the area around my feet.

I began to feel like I was in a stupor, not really knowing what I was doing or why I was doing it, but I continued to listen intently to the voice while inspecting the sidewalk. I noticed the cement block I was standing on was newly finished, smooth and seemingly perfect. I looked ahead a foot or so to the next section of the walk and saw that this block had a few blemishes and cracks.

I continued to look forward as I walked on repeating the process. I saw other blocks with imperfections and then I walked up to a section where the walk was filled with cracks, flaws and broken cement. As I looked closer, the cause of the problem was raised roots from a tree extended and growing underneath causing the cement to crack, split and break the walkway. If the roots continued growing it would affect other areas of the walk. Going on, I kept looking and saw the rest of the walkway heading to my house was smooth and even.

As I turned back and looked at the path of the sidewalk, I wondered what it all meant. The voice spoke and said "This is your life". Each section of the sidewalk represented a portion of my life. The tree was deeply rooted, alive and growing. The roots needed to be removed to prevent damage, only then could the walk be repaired.

This is what I felt based on what I observed and, at this point, I had no idea that in order to fix my life I needed to remove the sin and any unhealthy habits from me. Bad things had taken deep root in my life as I journeyed towards my eternal home. Over the years, I had done a great job trimming back the tree here and there and replacing the sidewalk, but the roots kept growing back, causing my issues to reappear over and over again. My selfishness was so absorbed it nearly destroyed me on many occasions.

Our move was finally complete. Home Sweet Home... 452 East Eagle Lane. Yes! We were all moved in and one big happy family - mom, dad, my brother John, plus my three younger sisters, Lori, Marsan and Susan.

Our home was beautiful and spacious - my parents had a master bedroom with all the fixings, Marsan and Susan shared a room, Lori had her own and John and I shared a room. We had a full size basement, a huge garage and attic. The house had a den that led to an attached enclosed patio, out to a gigantic yard with an industrial size swing set, and my dad had an independent basketball court built just for my brother. It was something you would see at a neighborhood elementary school. The house sat on a slight hill with a large walnut tree and a long driveway lead from the street to our garage. Dad drove a brand new copper-colored Lincoln Continental Mark 4 for business and an El Camino for work; mom had a station wagon.

We were the first and only black family in our neighborhood that consisted of prominent lawyers, doctors and surgeons, influential real estate representatives and stockbrokers. There were also independent business owners that made their fortunes in everything from masonry to furniture stores.

I had the privilege of growing up with their children and living in an affluent environment, attending a predominately white school called Montgomery Elementary.

After going through admissions with my parents, it was determined I needed to repeat the second grade. I was ok with that and did not make a fuss; I really wanted to get started with school. I made friends very easily and my award-winning personality went over great with my teachers. I was helpful, polite and well mannered. I was affectionately called "Fat Ronnie", a nickname given because there were 3 Ronnie's in our family and I was the only fat one.

One of my favorite pastimes and highlights of my day was

lunchtime. The school cafeteria allowed you to bring your bag lunch or purchase the school lunch, and sometimes I did both. They even offered almost every day my all-time favorite… cookies!

Apparently, I was not alone and cookies were a favorite for two of my classmates as well. These little girls must have been fascinated with my presence. I am thinking it may have been my six-inch afro, the only "fro" in the crowd. The girls signed up for the school's welcoming committee and wanted me to receive their gifts. Innocently, they snuck up behind me with their giddy laugh, but I ignored them because I was enjoying myself in a milk and cookie zone. Suddenly, cookie crumbs from heaven showered over me, and all I could think of was why would anyone waste crumbs on my hair.

I knew the girls were having fun and really meant no harm. I was already programmed to handle events like this. I was told not to start fights, but I could certainly finish them. The only problem was that my mental CPU was not programmed on how to deal with girls, and to top things off I was embarrassed and could not compute rejection on any level.

Since just about everyone in the cafeteria saw what happened, I became the center of attention and they were laughing… Ok, now I have to deal with the problem. Maybe this was just a big mistake and someone will come over to me, apologize, give me a hug and then I will feel better and this whole thing will go away. Well, none of that happened so Ronald James went into action; I had to teach these girls a lesson - not to mess with the "Bro's Fro".

After a few minutes, the girls returned to their seats and began whispering to each other, I calmly walked behind them, placed my left hand on one of the girls head and my right on the other girls head, introduced myself by smashing their heads together like two brass symbols in a marching band. Suddenly, the laughing stopped and all eyes were on me as I was quickly introduced to the principal, who just happened to be one of the girls' father. I was suspended for two days. It was during this time I began to be singled out, not because I was black, but because I felt everyone thought there was something wrong with me.

Both my school friends and those in the neighborhood told me I was different. I walked and talked funny, so I dropped everything I could that associated me with being different, including me being black. At this stage in my life, if it was possible for me to change my skin color, I would have in order to avoid rejection and be able to fit in.

Unfortunately, I did not know how to talk or express my feelings about this to anyone, so I made the proper adjustments to what I could change – my speech and my walk. I got rid of the slang of Ebonics, changed my hook and movements, and adopted a new kind of swagger. As the habit became second nature to me, this added to my dilemma because I became good at reading and mimicking my surroundings.

When it was time to visit my grandparents in the old neighborhood in Philly, my peers turned into my critics and told me I sounded like a white boy. They were very swift and harsh with their judgment, so I had to do something fast to avoid a problem that seemed to be recurring.

I found myself experiencing that familiar feeling of being out of place while in my own skin, and this time with my own kind. I felt different and, once again, rejected.

In times past, I have heard it said, "While in Rome, do as the Romans do", so I switched back to my old ways and acted like those around me. I switched back and forth so often it became second nature. I learned to change my mannerisms, facial looks and expressions, talk, walk, and my attitude. The effects also caused me to learn how to change my emotions and how I felt inside. I became a chameleon on two feet.

This hindered my growth as a young man because I never allowed those around me a chance to bear witness to my true self or my feelings. I could mask with perfection and what a person saw in me was what I allowed them to see.

A situation happened to me when I was in the fourth grade. My teacher asked me to stand up in front of my class and read a requested portion of a story. As I read, I began having a difficult time with the flow and pronunciation of words and some of my fellow classmates begin to snicker; in my mind it seemed as if it was the whole class.

I reacted by closing my book, slamming it on my desk and telling my teacher that I was not going to read anymore. I decided right then and there that reading was not fun and I hated it. Just like that, I stopped reading…and it took more than twelve years for me to pick up another book and read cover to cover.

I was frustrated and chose to shut the door on Ronald James and his true feelings. I gave no further explanation concerning the matter. I thought by not reading I was getting back at them for laughing at me …when in reality, I was the only one being hurt. For years, I carried this type of resentment around, and only now have I learned that no one else was hurt by it except me.

I felt I had a decent childhood and considered it safe, enjoyable and normal, for the most part, especially since the move to the suburbs. Now that we were living in the neighborhood of "the Jones'", I had to do my best to keep up with the "little Jones'", you know, the children of the prominent lawyers, doctors and surgeons, influential real estate representatives and stockbrokers …so when my peers got motorcycles, I needed one too! All I had to do was drop the question to my dad. I built up the nerve and blurted out, "Dad, will you ever get me that motorcycle I asked you about? My dad came back with a question of his own, "Can you spell 'motorcycle' for me?" I gave it my best shot, but failed, so I asked my mom to help with the spelling and she was happy to do me the honors. My dad added that as soon I could spell the word on my own, I would get that motorcycle.

Mom and I went over the word a few times and it did not take me long to memorize the spelling. Memorizing was easier than learning; little did I realize that I was setting myself up for later life skills. I worked hard because I knew that, at the end of this effort, I would receive a prize.

My dad came home one day fussing as he walked through the door. I was called to address the messy garage. It was my job to keep the garage clean and in order, but I did not understand what he was complaining about since I had just been out there cleaning the day before. I was always on top of my duties, chastised enough to know that it needed to be done correctly, so that is always how I did it. I tried to explain that I had just cleaned the garage, but Mom chimed in and told me not to talk back to my father. I was confused about what was going on and wanted to speak my mind.

She directed me to go to the garage to see what mess my dad was talking about. When I opened the door from our den leading to the garage, there it was - my motorcycle! My parents had tricked me, but the payoff was great and I was overjoyed. I jumped on to try it out; I was ready to ride!

After school the following day, I took my bike out for a test run. I drove my motorcycle everywhere that my feet could not take me, traveling with or without my friends. Inspired by the freedom, I went in any and all directions and the independence was exciting.

I believe it was around the sixth grade when I began to see the big picture that the world did not revolve totally around Ronald James. My sixth grade teacher helped me to look beyond myself, and again I was faced with life questions, only this time it was asked by my teacher and not my inner voice.

He presented the question, "Are you here because of chance or because of purpose?" As a class, our teacher wanted to know our thoughts on the subject and made it an open discussion. Was life all about chances? Was it chance we were raised in the United States? Was it because of a specific purpose that our ancestors landed on the shores of this nation? Was it chance or purpose that we were born to our parents?

These and other questions were thought provoking. Our teacher was really preparing us for the future. We talked about the arrival of the year 2000 and things we may be doing by that time. We talked about politics, interracial marriage, the stock market and the economy.

The class was very interesting and it challenged me to do something I loved, which was brainstorming and growing intellectually. I felt like I was all grown up; however, things were about to change.

One day my mom and her friends were gathered in the kitchen casually chatting when she asked me to do something. My reaction was a smart remark out of my mouth, "yeah right". The next thing I knew, she picked up a spoon and hit me. Well, it did not hurt, and I thought it was funny so I started laughing.

Mom did not take a liking to my sense of humor and neither did any of her friends who, by displaying their dissatisfaction, only added fuel to my mother's fire. They were rolling their eyes, sucking their teeth and hissing like alley cats, shaking their heads in disbelief.

Clearly, this was the wrong day and the wrong crowd for me to be acting up. Testing my mom in front of her friends was not a good move on my part. I crossed the line and was disrespectful to her. I never saw the death stare because she blew right past that and jumped on me with all fours like a lioness attacking a young wildebeest in the wild.

Things happened so fast I had no time to apologize, let alone get out of her way. I was hit with a flurry of Muhammad Ali combos; blows were landing upside my head as though she was floating like a butterfly and stinging ME like a bee!

I went down for the count, and her friends gave their sign of approval as they were shaking their heads with satisfaction on my mother's behalf. As far as they were concerned, momma handled her business! I got up from the kitchen floor dazed, shocked and embarrassed, with her friends laughing and saying, "Um-hum Miriam, you did right!"

Up until this point in my life, my dad tolerated my actions and the behavior I displayed, but my life was about to take a drastic turn for the worse.

I chose to get into a fight with a boy who lived across the street. Another stupid fight for another stupid reason, but I thought he deserved it. A neighbor came to break it up and I cursed him out like nobody's business when he said he was calling my parents. I figured I would go home and if anything came out of the situation, I would deal with it then. Most likely I would get fussed at by mom, and then later by dad when he came home from work.

To my surprise, my dad was already there…and so was the report of the fight! The neighbor I cursed out had made good on his promise and phoned my parents. This was not a day of good choices.

Dad went ballistic, out of control and in a fit of rage; he cursed and yelled at the top of his voice. I had never seen actions displayed like this by anyone before, especially from my dad. He was very theatrical, appearing as though he was a caged wild animal.

I was not paying attention to what he was saying because I focused only on his body language, knowing his frustrations were directed solely towards me from the poor choices I had just made.

With his eyes focused on me, I knew I was truly in trouble, continuing to step back as he advanced closer to me until my back was against the living room wall. I had nowhere to go as dad got in my face and, sensing his anger, I am sure my expression revealed my fear.

By this time, my mom tried to get involved but she was a step too late. Dad punched me directly in my chest. The force of the blow was as if I was a grown man or worse…his enemy. This was a first, because I never experienced anything like this in my relationship with my dad. The wind was knocked completely out of me. I went down after doubling over and I could not breathe. All I remember from that point was my mom jumping between us holding dad back from doing any further damage.

Dad was acting strange in his behavior that day, and the days following were questionable, too. He began missing days at home, sometimes weeks at a time, and when he did come around, it was only to gather clothes, cash, and jewelry. Later on, he came for the cars.

I was in the seventh grade when dad bailed out, cashing in his chips, splitting, and running off with no explanation. My mother shared years later that dad had been running around on her with one of his barmaids.

He had been heavily involved with alcohol, marijuana and heroin. He collected all the cash from all of his businesses and allowed them to fold, including the rental properties AND our home on Eagle Lane, which went into foreclosure. Yes… foreclosure. We were literally forced onto the streets.

I realize none of this was my choice, but I wonder if some of my choices did not strain my parent's relationship. I also realize that after this happened, I had the opportunity to make better choices in order to help my mother maintain the lifestyle she had been used to. However, I was too selfish for that and made the choices that benefitted me the most. Unfortunately, most of those choices did not benefit others in the least.

Mom did not want us to move back to the city of Philadelphia, so she, a kept woman and housewife, began to fight for herself and the well-being of her five children. She was determined to provide the best for all of us no matter what, and she set her goal that we would graduate from the same area high school, educated and with diplomas. She did what was necessary and two, sometimes three jobs to keep us above water. She made selfless choices.

I had so many unanswered questions. Why was my life turning into such disarray? Why this? Why now? Was there something wrong with me? Why did my dad pack up and walk out on my mother and our family?

People like my Aunt Bev tried encouraging me, telling me that once I accepted Jesus Christ into my life, everything was going to change…at least that is what I thought. My aunt's church was a large Baptist church on Wayne Avenue in the Germantown section of Philadelphia. That is where I accepted Christ back in 1975. My life was changing all right, but it appeared to be for the worst.

The preacher asked was there anyone in the congregation that particular Sunday who wanted a change that day, anyone willing to have Jesus as his Lord and Savior? I heard the call from that small voice inside of me and this time it cried out "Yes", as my insides yearned for a change.

The next thing I knew, my hand went straight up and I was ushered to the front of the church, and then lead to the back where someone asked me a series of questions and read some verses from the bible. It was then I asked Jesus to come into my heart. On this day, the preacher had my undivided attention by telling everyone in the congregation he was proud of me for stepping up and coming forward. God had a very special call and plan for my life, but I began feeling both encouraged and confused. What would God want with me and when is this special thing suppose to happen, if at all? "Hello Mr. God… when are the heavens going to open up and your angels descend upon me and say, 'this is your purpose Ron James'?"

No, I did not see any lights, sparks or flashes, nor did I witness some great miracle that would lead me to believe "Ronald James, this is it!" As a matter of fact, things seemed to be closing in on me, especially at school.

I made myself hate anything that had to do with reading just because of what happened to me in the fourth grade. The door was open for me to cheat and that is exactly what I did. In order to survive in the classroom, I became a master cheater by spending more time and energy concentrating on the movements of my teachers rather than studying for their tests.

When my teachers turned their backs or became

preoccupied with classroom matters, I went to work allowing my eyes to roam. It did not matter what type of test I faced – multiple choice, fill in the blanks or essays – I was able to take a mental photograph of what was before me and study my classmates answer sheet. For those who sat close enough to me, I would read a few lines of the question from the essay, then look at the opening and closing statements from classmate's assignment and brainstormed to put something together for the middle.

I perfected this style of cheating just to receive the grades good enough to pass. I began to realize something very valuable was happening because of this habit. I was developing life skills. I learned I could remain calm while under extreme pressure, able to watch and read peoples actions without allowing them to know I was studying them. I would go unnoticed and, in a lot of cases, I could predict their actions; this would help determine my movements.

I am not condoning this character trait, nor do I believe that cheating is the way to go. I could have learned to observe people in a different way; however, this is what seemed to happen and what worked for me. Now that cheating was added to my portfolio of character defects, it seemed to work together in conjunction with everything else and, without notice, my life was spiraling more and more off course.

By the tenth grade I was allowed to "taste" as mom would say. As long as I drank at home it was okay with her. I enjoyed drinking and the taste of an ice cold beer. After slamming one down, I found pleasure from the long belch that erupted seconds after consuming a can, not to mention the buzz and tingling feeling I felt. Let there be no mistake about it, alcohol became my "wonder serum."

After drinking one or two beers, I became extremely

focused. Instead of my mind racing from subject to subject, which seemed to be my norm, I now zoomed intently on what was at hand. Alcohol appeared to give me a 'Webster's Dictionary' vocabulary that sounded like poetic justice... and if nothing else, it made complete sense to me. I gained courage to converse with girls. I was able to tell people just how I felt. I pursued any materialistic thing I wanted, and became cynical in the process.

Hands down, alcohol allowed me to escape from any pain, embarrassment, guilt, hurt, shame or fears I faced. I am not sure how my alcohol use affected others, but it helped me to think clearly and I learned to use it to my advantage. I let nothing stand in my way to have access to money, women, power and drugs.

For the most part, I could get along with anyone, unless you chose to belittle me by speaking in a condescending manner. I developed an ability to adjust my personality in order to compliment and fit with any group I was in, regardless of our differences. This gave so much more freedom in allowing me to travel from circle to circle and blend in; as long as there was a group, I was networking. Alcohol helped me to ride each wave. I thought I was finally growing up and maturing in many aspects of my life; however, there was still room for growth and development in other areas.

There was a time my mom decided to spot-check my bedroom and I could not figure out for the life of me what she was looking for. I was not into drugs. She knew I kept a few Playboy or Penthouse magazines around, and if I wanted a beer, all I had to do was ask. Something was up because very rarely did she come up to my room for anything, even just to check on me. Although, this particular day she showed up in rare form and was searching for something.

At age sixteen, I thought I knew everything there was to know about life, so how could my mom possibly know what she was doing? I shared some of my thoughts and feelings with her in order to try and help her find whatever it was that she was looking for. It was very clear we were not on the same page.

I watched my mom, the Matriarch, Mimi, the Queen, transform into Attila the Hun right before me. As she was making tracks towards me with a full head of steam, being the quick thinker that I am, I figured I would push the envelope with her since I had nothing to lose. We were already engaged in an adult conversation, plus it was very clear she was about to work the motherly move on me, so I chose to get her to listen to reason. I told her I would kill myself by jumping out of the window from my third story room. I must have gotten her attention because she stopped dead in her tracks. Ha, it worked!

She began to smile as she stood for a few seconds before she walked over to the window and opened it. Standing like Vanna White on Wheel of Fortune, she pointed to the window, as if it was the next letter in the phrase that said, "Go Ahead and Jump". Well, I guess my mom knew something after all because I was not about to jump, and she went on about her business as she walked away and out of my room, laughing even though she never did find what she was looking for. No matter how foolish I was at times, mom always had my back without hesitation…and I had hers.

One night, I came home from hanging out with the boys and I did my regular routine of hitting the kitchen for something to snack on – hot dogs being among my favorites. I noticed our next door neighbor was over for a visit and was chatting with mom. Their cigarettes were lit and they were sipping their drinks. The neighbor's nephew was seated at the table with them. I greeted everyone as I proceeded to fix my food - I needed something in my gut to even out the alcohol.

After I ate, I went to the living room where my brother John laid stretched out on the sofa watching TV. We talked for a while, which was one of those rare brother-to-brother conversations where we both just enjoyed each other's company. I grabbed a quilt and stretched out on the carpet in front of the sofa.

All was well until I heard my mother's distress as she screamed and the bench she was sitting on was dragged across the kitchen floor. It may have taken a total of three seconds for me to jump to my feet, leap clear over my brother and move through the living and dining rooms to get to the kitchen.

As I approached the scene, there was only one thing on my mind and that was to IMMEDIATELY resolve any issue that was bringing discomfort to my mom. My target was the nephew and I was on my way to shut him down.

As I entered the kitchen and saw him towering over my mother with his fist clenched, she was curled up with her hands up in the air covering her face. She had slid all the way to one end of the bench and was pinned in the corner.

Now ask yourself one simple question....what would you do? Someone is about to do bodily harm to someone you love....yea, you got my point! I trashed this guy! I cold-cocked this joker right upside his head, sending him into the next week to enjoy a dream. I knocked him clean out and he never saw it coming. His head hit the floor and his body lay motionless in a peaceful state.

However, I was still in attack mode and was moving quickly to stomp him and give him the rest of what he had coming, but mom had other ideas. She jumped from the bench to her feet and grabbed my arm and in a stern, yet sweet tone said, "Ronnie, it's okay." I looked her in the eyes and the connection was made.

At the same time, our neighbor begged me not to do any more damage. I looked in her direction, smiled to let her know that she was heard, and out of respect for her, I retracted. I turned back to my mom and gave her a frown, my scowl of disapproval was a look only she was able to see and understand. Our neighbor dragged her nephew back home and that was that. My brother never moved off the sofa. Later mom asked him "What happened to you?" John said, "I knew Ronnie was going to handle it." I was becoming a man, at least I sure felt like one, especially now that mom and I had an understanding.

I was a man all right, but only because I had the option to piss against a wall. I was without honor, integrity, honesty, and becoming heartlessly selfish. I would piss on you and tell you not to worry because it is just rain. I stole from my family, friends, anybody and anyone, and that included the helpless and the dead.

My loving grandfather was diagnosed with colon cancer and died suddenly. Both my mom and grandmother took his death very hard. My grandmother moved in with us and our family rallied around her in support, everyone except yours truly. While family comforted her, I saw a golden opportunity to snoop and rummage through my grandfather's personal property.

Yes, I chose to go to a forbidden place when we went to my grandparent's house and steal from the man who demonstrated the love and kindness a grandparent should. I showed my appreciation by robbing them. I was skilled in my pursuits. I slipped into their room and began uncovering and opening things, searching very swiftly through his belongings.

My actions went undetected and, as I focused on my surroundings, I kept my ears opened for any unexpected interruptions. I had acquired this skill at a young age while looking at porn in the basement of the White House on Wanamaker Street.

My grandparent's bedroom was like treasure hunting to me. I found shoeboxes, cigar boxes and many other boxes of all shapes and sizes scattered throughout the room.

As I opened each box, I was surprised to find a variety of items hidden away from sight. There were Susan B. Anthony dollars, all kinds of change jars, x-rated playing cards, porn, gold teeth, gold fillings, jewelry, pictures, letters, books - you name it and it seemed to be there. I even found a silver .38 revolver.

After taking what I wanted, or better yet plundered what I felt would benefit me, I took the loot with me to a coin shop at the local mall that brought gold, silver and coins in exchange for cash. What a man I was.

My life started to repeat itself by doing the same things over and over again; a vicious cycle that only seemed to get worse. The summer of 1980 did not end without a major incident. It was back to school time and, of course, I would need to have the latest gear. I decided to go up to the local mall and execute my plans of retail theft, only this time I dragged along a young neighborhood friend for the mission. He always looked up to me so why not show him just how easy it was to steal.

Our mission began in one of the men's clothing stores and I proceeded to put my plan into full action. I spotted a shirt that caught my eye, located my size and quickly went into the dressing room and stuffed the shirt in my pants.

On my way out of the store, the manager looked straight at me, standing between my getaway exit and me. He was not aggressive, not in the least, in fact, he was very smooth and simply asked if I could come back in and speak with him and I agreed – My second mistake. He said, "Let's talk over here at my desk," and then calmly said, "Please sit down." - My third mistake.

As I sat down, he started off by telling me how well mannered I was, something I already knew about myself. He asked me for my name and where I was from – My fourth mistake. Then the manager switched gears and said, "Look, just give back the shirt and get the hell out my store." I thought to myself that this gig is up and I will have to give him the shirt and get out of there, so I pulled the shirt out of my pants and gave it to the manager. The entire time my young mentee and friend witnessed the event and I am sure this made an impact for him not to steal.

After handing over the shirt, the manager informed me the police were on their way and I could not leave. But wait a minute! I was lied to and tricked into believing I was going to walk out of that store scot-free.

Oh, and if you are wondering what my first mistake was… It was on September 3, 1980 thinking I could go into someone's establishment and pull off the perfect crime. This was the first of a plethora of conscious mistakes I chose to make that landed me in custody to be processed, photographed, fingerprinted and questioned.

This was my first arrest. Now, with the results of my life choices becoming crucial, you would think my CPU upstairs would cause me to change course, but it was not as easy as that.

It was during this time the father of one of my friends allowed me to work with them cleaning offices for their janitorial service company. No matter how kind and thoughtful they were, my focus and agenda remained constantly on me …and how did I repay them? I stole things from the very offices we cleaned.

One day, in the presence of his son, the father asked me if I picked up a stethoscope from one of the doctor's offices we cleaned. Of course, I said, "No"! The one reason I felt he did not push the issue and chose to believe me is because the first time I met them a few years back, they invited me to go Christmas holiday shopping and I spotted a man who dropped his wallet. I picked it up, told my friend's dad, and pointed out the man. The wallet was returned and everyone was grateful, so how could he think that I would steal anything now.

Then one day when we were cleaning an office, my friend pulled a rag out of his pocket and along with it came a $10 bill. It landed on the floor, but my friend's back was turned and I did not think twice about picking it up and placing it in my pocket. Not only did I steal from the office, I stole from my friend as well.

As I look back, I am not sure if that specific incident was a test of my integrity or if my friend ever shared it with his dad, but none of that really mattered. Ron James was about to be seen by the world.

My actions spoke louder than anything that came out of my mouth. My thievery continued to show its ugly face wherever I went. I looked for any angle to beat the system, 24/7, and I slowly developed a mindset of getting over on everything and everyone. My self-centeredness led me to believe I could do or say anything I pleased. I considered myself an opportunist who thrived on ways to get over on people.

I knew that our high school kept a display case full of all kinds of desirable candies and keepsakes. While in school one day, I saw an open door of opportunity and went through with my plan to slide the lock along the glass edge to jimmy it open wider; helping myself to the contents of the case. Someone spotted me and I got caught. I confessed and told my version of what took place...receiving only a slap on the hand.

This idea of acting as though I am totally honest when I get caught always seemed to get me out of whatever trouble I was in; therefore, allowing me to get off light with punishment. I had no idea I was digging myself deeper and deeper into a web I would not be able to get out of on my own free will.

What high school story would be complete without a prom? It was my senior prom night and I stopped by to see my mom, pick up my prom date and then meet up with the rest of our party. I was quite the gentleman by opening doors for her. I was polite, courteous and soft spoken. We ate at one of the finest restaurants in the area, and the only difference between the kindness I showed her and the kindness she showed me was that I had selfish motives.

For the first time in my life, this young lady treated me like a king. I was receiving what I needed from someone who was willing to play her role, so why was I ready to sabotage this relationship?

After eating we joined our classmates at the prom. We danced, socialized and I sported my trophy on my arm. We got in line, had our picture taken, and suddenly my insides ran cold. I was turned off by how the picture turned out and placed the blame squarely on her. Our photograph appeared as if she was frowning or upset about something when, in reality, she may have been caught off guard. Whatever the case, it was not intentional on her part; however, I labeled it as such. So even though I was planning an exit strategy from this relationship, we enjoyed a few more dances and then it was off to Atlantic City for more partying into the wee hours of the morning.

It was early in the morning when I got back to where I lived in North Wales, PA. My date was curled up next to me on the front seat when I spotted something very unusual. On the side of the road I saw a station wagon turned on its side in a ditch. I mean the wheels of the vehicle were off the road and in the air. I heard that small voice inside telling me to stop and see what was going on.

I pulled over, jumped out of my car and hopped onto the station wagon to investigate the situation. It was clear to me what was wrong. There was an older man, approximately in his sixties, who was helplessly drunk and stuck in his car. He had run off the road after God only knows how many drinks from one of the local clubs, and now he was impaired and immobilized. I opened his door, pulled him out and my date helped me load him into our car. I figured out where he lived and drove him to his house.

I genuinely felt a connection with this man, almost like I was meant to see him when I did, like a fore-telling of my life to come, so to speak. I felt good about helping him and I wanted nothing in return. I could see that my date was very pleased with my actions and it boosted her impression of me. However, she had no idea that this act of kindness was the only one that she would ever witness. Yes, it was real and from my heart, so why could I not be like this to everyone?

I could tell that her feelings toward me were increasing

and this allowed us to enjoy each other physically once again on my mother's sofa. I drove her home and thought that was the end; what else was there? I got what I wanted, right?

Well, I did not even have the decency to be a man and call her to say thanks or explain my abrupt departure…instead she called me over and over again, wondering why I would not answer. She called so much and so often, I finally told my mom to handle it because I wanted nothing to do with her. The excuse I gave and ran with was that she purposely tried to ruin my night by making an ugly face when it came time to take my one and only prom picture. That was my story and I was sticking to it.

This young lady had no idea I was lying on her to everyone I talked to. All I wanted to do was move on with my life. This break up event caused that sweet young girl so much stress that she ended up in the hospital. My mom shared this news with me as if this would change my feelings. The truth was that I could have cared less.

After she realized it was over, she called to see if it would be all right for my mom to at least send her a prom picture of us together. I told mom to do whatever she wanted to do and that I was done with her. It was crazy how I honestly and sincerely cared more about a drunken man I found in a ditch, not knowing him from a can of paint, than I did this young girl.

Perhaps to him, I must have been an angel of light. However, on the flip side, there was that sweet someone who gave of herself in every possible way for my happiness and, in return, I treated her like crap…and to make matters worse, I manipulated others into believing my lies. Distributing unwarranted hurt, as though I were an angel of darkness.

*I have never met a man who has given
me as much trouble as myself*

-D. L. Moody

CHOICE TWO
ME

I FELT SAD KNOWING that it was time to move on to our twelfth grade graduation. Some would leave friends and family to go into the armed services, others would go to work or travel and a large percentage of my classmates went on to college, including me.

Yes, it was time for my college debut. All of the entrance exams were complete, my paperwork for admission was sent and I received my letter of acceptance from Brandywine College. Next my application fees, Pell Grant, student loan and all of my financial obligations were in order, and I even had enough money to open a savings account.

My wardrobe was freshly pressed and up to date; I said all of my goodbyes and off to school I went. Now, when I walked through the doors of Brandywine College, I came with the idea of integrity; my intent was to adhere to all of the rules. I was going to make a concerted effort to have an open mind in learning and understanding, while applying my knowledge to work with the curriculum. That meant no to plagiarism, unethical or dishonest practices or cheating of any kind. I wanted to do the work on my merit; receiving the grades that reflected my most sincere efforts. This was my game plan, but sometimes in life your best is not good enough.

I found the college pace to be fast and my pace to be slow. I was fine with my math courses, but when it came to everything else I needed help. My pride did not allow me to say "Hey, I really should not be here people - my reading comprehension and speed is on a fourth grade level" Why? Because I gave up reading and my dedication was a big zero. Not to mention that my writing skills were awful, as was my sentence structure, grammar, punctuation... and my spelling was hideous.

It did not take Ronald James long to figure out he needed to revise his plan. I had concluded the need to "cheat my ass off" in order to catch up with my classmates.

I began to stereotype those I wanted to cheat from. I leaned more towards those who were white; subconsciously, I felt that black people were not as smart. Of course, I knew that I was black and by no means did I consider myself to be dumb, nor did I look at my parents or any of my boys as lacking intelligence. No, somewhere along the line, I picked up this mindset during my childhood through some type of subliminal messages.

As for cheating, I found it easier to do in college. I specialized in using my personality as leverage in networking and making friends. Once I befriended you, I used you and made it hard for people to tell me no. This played into my social role on campus.

It was only a week into the first semester and I tried to hit all the parties. There was a party of some kind, for some reason, some place each and every night of the week. On occasion, the party would carry over into the next day or start up the next night where it left off.

Brandywine College was a party school and there were parties in the campus townhouses on any given floor of the

3-story dorms, and even in the recreation center called "The Barn". The promoters of such events were the fraternities, sororities and other social groups located on the campus.

All of them competed for bragging rights and pledges by giving the biggest and best parties. Plus, none were lacking amenities and it was at one of those parties that I was introduced to "grain punch".

I knew from the start not to go too far with this stuff, and that after just one cup full of this fruity drink, I started to feel its effects. Not only was I certain anyone else who drank this and felt anything like I did should stop, they should have known something was up.

I was told later the punch had been laced with lemon drops, better known as 714 Quaaludes, which is a toxic combination. The mixture of grain alcohol and Quaaludes would set unsuspecting people, mainly females, up for a sexual encounter. Sometimes welcomed, but often times not.

It did not take me long to hook up with a young lady. I met this girl at one of the parties and invited her back to my room. We enjoyed each other's company and the time we spent was short and sweet. We said our goodbyes that night and that was it, there were no strings attached…so I thought.

We went on about our lives; however, she had left a little something behind. The following day I noticed an itch around my jock area and this itch lasted well into the second and third day. As it became worse, I tried jock itch cream and even hot showers, but the itch intensified. I had to get to the bottom of this, so I went to the bathroom with a hand mirror, angling it so I could examine and investigate. HELP! I was being eaten alive by what seemed like thousands of tiny insects.

I panicked and called my roommate into the bathroom and asked him what the hell was going on. He busted out laughing and told me I had the crabs. Well, I was not in any mood for jokes, so I went straight to the medical office and the campus nurse was not surprised. She serviced me with a smile and some quill shampoo that ended my itch problem. I thought to myself how could such a pretty girl pass bugs? After that, I did not see her again nor did I ever want to.

Then came the day when there was a meeting for anyone who was interested in playing basketball for the college. I was one of those interested so I met with the coach. During try-outs I did my best to do as instructed - I was a fundamental player with a basic game and could hustle. I did well in high school and felt I could add something to the team.

The coach recognized I possessed leadership skills, which I never realized about myself. He pulled me aside, complimented my efforts, and then asked if I would be interested in being co-team captain along with another player. I said yes! I was grateful, yet confused because I was used to being second, always second, and always a support player to the team.

However, not with Coach, he wanted me out front. My mom always told me that I would get my day in the sun, my day to shine and it looked like the day was finally here.

Our team played hard and we had our good moments, and finally my dream came true. During one of our home games, I snatched the ball off the glass and pushed it out to my boy, who kicked it out to our point guard, and with a no-look bounce pass between his legs, he set the ball hurling out ahead of me as I slashed to the basket filling the lane. I was able to get my hands on the ball and, without thinking, I took two steps and sailed in for the slam dunk.

The exhilaration I felt far surpassed my expectations; I had arrived. I was young, horny, and totally out of control. I was a leader all right, the ring-leader of the spotlight who was always looking to cash in on any and all opportunities that presented themselves.

One day, three of my friends and I wanted to have a drinking contest. The lethal combination of ego and testosterone made drinking contests frequent and easy to start. The other essential ingredients were half kegs of Milwaukee's finest, funnels, shots and our favorite 32 oz Dollar Store glass mugs.

Shortly into this 4-man party – like just after two drinks - one of my friends and I, who were both notorious lightweights, decided to get something to eat. Sparked by an alcohol-induced stroke of genius, and with the assistance of a lookout, we broke into the college cafeteria and helped ourselves to whatever we wanted.

This became my routine as if I was perfectly within my rights. That was the funny thing about alcohol in my system. It enabled me to do things that I would not do sober. Namely to fulfill greedy, lustful desires; with practice and familiarity, my mindset became more fixed, my actions more corrupt, and my justification more solid. I was getting what I wanted and that was the goal. The trend for me was beyond the normal right-of-passage associated with college.

Although this particular mayhem was interwoven in me, my path was darker and I was in deeper than I realized. Road trips and frat parties were the norm. One of my boys always picked me up in his car – a big, old passed down Chevy Impala that was perfect for our purposes of heading to other campuses.

Drexel, Temple, Widener and West Chester all became regular stomping grounds. Being out and about on newly conquered territory only further fueled how far I could take my indulgent, manipulative behavior. I would lie, steal, and do whatever I needed to achieve my goals, which typically involved excessive drinking and sex.

I had a constant tug of war raging within my soul between Bad Ron and Good Ron. It is no wonder a very close, special lady friend dubbed me with the pet name 'Ron-Ron'. The name stuck with me and became a campus nickname, mainly due to the crown I won when I entered the "Mr. Brandywine" contest on campus.

Yes, Ron-Ron was the King and it truly symbolized the duality of who I was becoming. One Ron - Good Ron - was fair, sensitive, honest, generous and supportive, but he was also afraid of being hurt and hid that fear of rejection and embarrassment deep within. The other Ron - Bad Ron - was sinister and fiendish.

On the outside, Ron was on top of the world, but on the inside, Ron was experiencing toxic shame and guilt. I felt like a failure and no amount of alcohol could change the fact that I could not read, write or spell beyond the 4th grade. Alcohol served the purpose for momentary relief, but reality always came back and hit me square in the face.

Rejection, coupled with shame, was a fiery mix that caused me to resent the world and anyone who over played their own intelligence to expose or down play mine. This fed my excuse to lash out at or to harm others because 'people who hurt are hurting people'.

I went around trying to prove that I was smart and over achieved whenever I could. I found superiority in the mindset of getting over and being deceptive and manipulating. This became second nature to me and I thought I was right in my thinking. I went around campus sleeping with as many girls as I could because I treated sex as an extension of my hurt to self-serve.

I was running rampant, attending every party I could, and living for the affects of alcohol. I wanted alcohol to do to females what it did to me, which was gain the courage to say what I needed to get the girl in bed. Once a few drinks were in them, it was only a matter of time before they would indulge me in my selfish desires.

I was in love with hearing them say, 'Oh Ron-Ron…last night' and 'Oh Ron-Ron this morning'…Followed by a kiss or a question of did it really happen? And my answer was always yes, even if I could not remember myself.

For the most part, my first year at college ended smoothly. A number of good friends moved on and my grades were above average so life could not have been better. However, inside I was very unhappy.

No matter what seemed right on the outside, I still felt empty on the inside. Despite all my campus prestige - hearing the sound of people chanting my name, the women I slept with, the money in my pocket or even bright, brand new clothing – nothing helped me feel better about myself. What was happening? Something did not feel right and I felt I was missing life's purpose. Was there something more? Where was the voice I had always heard? Why was I not hearing it now? I needed something I could love with all my heart, and that something needed to love me back.

The summer of 1982 came and ended before I realized it; the first day of college was right around the corner. Brandywine College had now officially become Widener University, the student body was expanding, and new students poured in from everywhere.

As usual, basketball, parties and women were on my mind. Before the semester even began, I was blind-sided with the number of events that began to unravel; I was forced to make several changes.

One of my teachers pulled me aside because she wanted to work with me. She noticed I had a problem spelling very basic words. The first word she pointed out to me was the word 'friend'. I spelled it F.R.E.I.N.D. She was very patient and helpful, taking time out to explain I could easily remember the spelling of this word by placing the word "end" at the end. My teacher was kind and part of me felt pleased that someone was willing to spend special quality time with me. However, toxic shame took over, told me that I was a failure at life, and to protect myself from being embarrassed; it was time to become a better cheater.

Then I found out my financial situation had become unglued. I needed more funds or I had to give up my room and board. Financially, I was forced to make a move, so I got my things together, packed up, and moved back home with mom. I tried to get back and forth to campus the best way I could. My basketball coach came to my aid and I was able to catch rides with him during the week, but on the weekends, I just stayed on campus.

I knew enough people that I moved from room to room. I crashed on floors, sofas, chairs and of course, in any bed of any girl that would take me in. This obviously was not the smartest choice and so many things began to drastically change as I started partying more and more often.

I, along with over twenty other guys, joined in pledging of what was a fast-growing fraternity. This national fraternity had opened the door for us to have our own charter. Everyone who made it through the grueling initiation and hell week was eligible to be part of the best organizations on the planet, Sigma Pi. I was officially a Sigma Pi pledge.

As a pledge, we did the typical things that one might see on TV or in the movie *Animal House*. We acted as servants to any Sigma Pi brother, memorized the Greek alphabet, accepted bizarre challenges, drank until we were wasted, and even ate live things...well, if you consider goldfish a delicacy.

In any event, we subjected ourselves to an onslaught of verbal, physical, emotional and mental abuse that was constant and unpredictable. Each of us reported to an assigned Big Brother, who acted as a sympathetic liaison that helped neutralize the unavoidable, pure torment of initiation.

Despite the media hoopla, parties and negative publicity that most fraternities receive, Sigma Pi really stood for something fundamentally sound. They stood for service toward others, in hopes of helping and changing themselves and the communities.

This was not some hodge-podge of people thrown together to celebrate a good time, no way! Our founding fathers preached about values, morals and integrity, so instead of trying to shine and receive praise whenever I could, I chose to be a team player and leader. I then carried over the principles of basketball and the fraternity to help the less fortunate. I understood as pledges we needed to help one another to bring this large group together.

Now I am not claiming that I was unique or alone in my service toward these guys. Other men stepped up and played their roles allowing us to grow closer together. As pledges, we bought into the fraternity colors of purple and gold, which we sported all around campus. We encouraged and believed in each other, we were one body even though we came from different walks of life and possessed different gifts, traits, personalities and attitudes. We were a close knit family.

The last night of our pledge experience was PURE HELL!,

but no matter what was thrown at us, we overcame the obstacles – even the one and only infamous moat. The moat ran through the campus grounds. Even after being baptized in its ice cold frigid waters, the night went down as historic. We received a wooden paddle to the backside, learned the official handshake and we were now Widener's Sigma Pi's founding fathers.

A great part of the success of this achievement was credited to one of our own, Mr. Jay Dubbs, who was a law professor on campus for the Widener Law School. This honorary brother later became active with national and has done so much for the brotherhood as a mentor, friend and brother to many, and he also played a significant role in my life.

My go-for-it attitude was tainted with arrogance. The campus was in the midst of cleaning up the image that Brandywine College held. Now that the campus had changed over to Widener University, there was a strong presence of campus security. Due to the havoc I caused on campus, I knew I was overdue for an encounter of the worst kind.

The day came when I was under the influence of more than enough beers and shots from one of the wildest campus parties I had ever attended. I had more than I could handle and made a choice. I went right when I should have gone left …or was it the other way around? Anyway, I got caught sneaking a half keg of beer into one of the dorms….BUSTED!

After meeting with the dean, I was expelled from all campus activities with the exception of my classes. How could she do this? Did she not know who I was? The dean knew precisely who I was and this event caused her to take drastic measures for the betterment of the student body and the Widener name.

After that, I was forced to creep around the campus, the

same campus where everyone once chanted my name. I went from king to outcast. I quickly made allegiances with any and every one I could because I needed help. I needed people to be my eyes and ears on campus; it was apparent that, regardless of the Dean's decision, I was still going to be me.

I was upset with life and myself in general and I continued to make poor choices. I quit the basketball team right in the middle of the season, I started drinking more, I began experimenting with lightweight drugs, and continued chasing and accepting any girl who welcomed me into their room and gave me a place of refuge.

Back on campus, my popularity was running thin. I came to one of our Sigma Pi meetings half lit. The Sergeant of Arms did not see eye to eye with my negative behavior. I was out of line so he simply told me to get in line or get out.

Well, I did not mind following his last order; however, before leaving I pulled a very childish yet aggressive act while making my exit. I reached out with both hands, grabbed the edge of his desk and flipped it over with him in it. I was dead wrong and I did this in front of all my Sigma Pi brothers as they watched in disbelief.

This had some major repercussions – I was immediately placed on probation and threatened with being blackballed from the frat. Our meetings were usually fun and upbeat, yet we always followed a tight line of principles. A disruption alone could have placed me on probation, but to place my hands on a fellow brother was a cardinal sin and would not be tolerated.

Already faced with being banned from campus, my grades and classroom performance declining, and my attitude shoddy at best, I was now faced with being blackballed from the only group of men who accepted me for me. The same group of men who rallied behind me and supported me in all I did. The question I now asked myself was, "What would I do without them?"

I made my own bed and now it was time to get in it. Nevertheless, in order to be blackballed, it would take a majority vote, and the one thing I had in my favor was a true friend. He did what was called 'dragging the red herring'. He took time out to speak on my behalf, one brother at a time asking them to give me another chance. The main reason I am sure he did this was due to our friendship. I met with my frat brothers, gave them my 20-minute plea of mercy speech because I needed their support, and then was asked to leave the room while they deliberated. I knew that no man was an island, and I believed in the brotherhood.

Like most elections, voting was closed. Once the votes were in, it came down to the wire and I had weathered the storm - only to find out later through my one true friend that it was a split decision in my favor. This gave me a second chance and I was able to remain a Sigma Pi brother.

Was I happy? Hell no! Instead of being thankful, I resented the fact that everyone was not willing to put up with my BS – my thinking was WAY OFF.

Nothing seemed to put me in line and my antics progressed as it crossed the line from being funny to criminal. I continued my career as a thief, as if I had made it my vocation. I crept in any open dorm room and helped myself to whatever I wanted - alcohol, money and personal items were all there for the taking.

The weekends always proved more lucrative after a 'big dorm party' (which the university claimed we did not have any more) and it was easy pickings. I chose to wait until the hours of four to five in the morning to make my moves.

This way I could get around virtually undetected; if I did run across someone during these early hours, it was most likely an unattended female who was more than happy to have some fun with Ron-Ron.

It was time for finals and the close of another year. After two years of college, I thought it may be possible I would be eligible to graduate Widener University with an associate degree, but there was a problem.

I was about to flunk EnglishComp2. My teacher told me in very simple English... "Ronald James, you need an A on your final just to receive an overall grade point average of a 2.0."

She went on to explain that if I was lucky and received a B on her final I would get a 1.0 GPA or a D. The 1.0 or D would allow me to graduate; however, that grade would not be transferable. What in the world was I going to do?

I was in trouble mainly because I knew at best I could get a D on the final, which would amount to an overall GPA of...you guessed it a big fat F; meaning no degree for me. In addition, I could not cheat my way through this one. If I could, I would have had a better GPA in EnglishComp2 to begin with ...oh, if only I did things differently.

I sat, pondered, brainstormed, and wrecked my brain trying to come up with a solution as to how in the world I was going to get myself out of this one. Harry Houdini could not pull this one off. Yes, I was in trouble all right. However, there were still a few weeks before my finals started and I really wanted to graduate with a degree - not that the paper it was printed on meant anything - I just wanted to be the first one in my family to achieve this status.

Even though it was a façade, I knew my mom would be happy and proud of me, so I needed to come up with a plan sooner rather than later. I ended up getting frustrated and drank myself into a stupor…what better way to deal with problems?!

I knew somehow there was an answer to this puzzle, a solution, and I just had to come up with something. I continued brainstorming until I finally came up with an idea. I knew I was very good at moving all around the campus in a stealth mode, only now, I decided to raise the bar.

I started to watch those who were supposed to be watching me. Instead of hitting on some unsuspecting drunk person who forgot to lock their dorm room, I now checked the security personnel and learned their every move.

With my sights focused on the classroom building, a few beers in my system, and a wire coat hanger as my tool of choice, I went into action. As I approached the double glass doors on the side of the building, the night security lights exposed my reflection, so I knew I needed to act fast or I would be seen. Getting caught was not an option.

I quickly positioned the wire hanger between the doors at an angle and once in place, all I had to do was pull the hanger back towards me. This created a motion that pushed the handle down, opening the door for my speedy entrance.

Once I was in the building, I crept into the hallway where all of the teacher's offices were. All the offices where located together, separated only by cubicles. To my surprise, most of the doors were open and those that were not, were locked. Nothing left to do but scale a small wall and I was in – full access to all that I needed. I proceeded to rummage through all their drawers with one thing in mind – find the book with the grades.

I quickly located all my teacher's offices, starting first with my EnglishComp2 teacher; however, for some reason I could not find her grade book. This was the one class I needed, but reluctantly, I settled for those books I could find and simply adjusted my grades. If I had an 82 on a test, I changed it to an 88; if I had a 71, I changed it 79, 81, 89 or a 94. I left with no incident.

I repeated this process a few nights later, only this time I blessed anyone in my class that was a Sigma Pi brother or someone that I liked. Unknown to any of them and much to their surprise, I acted as their grade angel and I am certain there were a number of GPA's that went up.

On my third trip, I received a surprise myself. I entered the building as usual, only this time I could not locate 'old slew foot' – the same guard who busted me with the keg. When I finally heard him, it was too late. He was right up on me and my heart began to race…he was so close to me I could hear him breathing.

I had just entered the teacher's section, crouched down and remained completely still. As I watched his flashlight scan the area, maneuver past me and then guide him through to the exit, I remained so still that it was hard for me to move once he was gone. I knew right then that I needed a point man, so I decided to share the details about my actions and new intentions with my frat brother …yes, the real true friend who saved me from being blackballed.

As we planned our final trip to the classroom building, it was the weekend before our finals started. While everyone on campus was cramming, we were creeping. I knew every room and office in the building was on old slew foot's route, except for the mail/copy room. Then it hit me! If there was anything to get from this mission, I am sure it could be found there!

Except for one major problem – the door was locked. At the same time, my frat brother and I noticed a small opening at the top of the door towards the ceiling. Without even discussing it, we acted on impulse. Yes, that is right - the idea was to scale the door and disappear into the opening.

I am not sure who went over the wall, but when it was all said and done the door was opened and we immediately went over to the copier. We looked up and saw the jackpot! This was better than hitting triple 7's across the board on the progressive slots at Harrah's Casino.

Right in front of me were the mailboxes of each teacher for every class that was offered and then some. In each box contained several copies of each final exam for every class from every professor. I moved with precision as I helped myself to one copy out of each mail slot.

With finals in hand, we made a clean getaway back to the dorms. I could not believe we scored every final for that semester. This was monumental and called for a celebration of epic proportion. I was back on top. Ron-Ron had saved the day. I was a hero with an ice cold beer in one hand and my EnglishComp2 final in the other. I felt like I was on top of the world. I was certain to get an A on the final and a 2.0 overall GPA for the course.

I rounded up a few of my last minute cramming, bloodshot eyed, coffee-drinking friends who shared in my EnglishComp2 class and immediately they went to work – the entire test was set up in multiple choice. There were approximately 40 questions in all and they were all answered with special care.

Once the questions were complete, all I needed to do was copy each letter down and transfer them to my trusty cheat sheet and then I was set. Oh, how sweet I thought it was to cheat! I passed out all the other finals to anyone who wanted them while I sat back and enjoyed my triumph.

When Monday rolled around I was ready; I was eager to get this test underway and over with. I planned on taking my time and enjoying the 'A' I was about to receive. However, something went wrong, terribly wrong. If Murphy had a law, it fell into place once I completed the test. I realized that the last question left on my test was unanswered. Okay… no problem, I will just pull out the old cheat sheet and go over my answers. I understood now what was wrong.

Somehow when I transferred the answers from the test to my trusty cheat sheet, I missed a letter to one of the questions and, because I did not know the material, I could not line things up on the sheet. That is when I started second guessing myself and I began changing the answers. I panicked because I did not know if I messed up from the very start, in the middle or towards the end. My back was against the wall. I gave up trying to guess what was what and just turned in my test.

Later, when the results were in, my English teacher told me I just made it with the grade of a B- and I would be receiving a D from her for EnglishComp2. All was not lost and at least I would be able to graduate. At a time when I should have been elated, I was let down and disappointed in myself more so because I could not even cheat correctly.

It was May 1983 and time to put on those caps and gowns. My mom, family and friends were excited for me and attended the ceremony to support me. All the graduates were lined up and we were ready to go, and there I was with a big 'ole smile on my face and a flask full of Jack Daniels under my gown; dipping down every chance I could to take a swig.

Summer of 1983 – what a great time for me! Life sure seemed easy. I just landed a job with the Philadelphia Coca-Cola Bottling Company, a plant in North Wales, PA. I was hired as a route merchandiser. The position paid extremely well and I was literally ten minutes walking distance from my house. I was assigned my own company car so I could travel all around to the different supermarket locations. I got a chance to network with store owners and managers. My job was very challenging. For instance, I got to compete with other merchandisers from companies like Pepsi and Canada Dry. I set up store displays, price signs and got to talk junk when the competition showed up.

The name Coca-Cola meant something. It was prestigious and for the most part, working for them was like walking around with a badge of honor. It felt good. I got along well with the store managers, so when I needed my check cashed they leapt at the chance to accommodate my request.

Cashing corporate checks was never so simple. No lines, no inquiring tellers – just cash and go. This event opened a door to my understanding of presentation and the advantage of those things that were not so obvious. I was making great money, enjoying my summer job, and thrilled with life in general and the company of friends I was keeping.

My summer was well underway; however, I was still uncertain of what I would do next. Should I continue working, further my college education or find something else to do? I finally made my decision and submitted all the necessary paperwork, met my financial obligations with student loans, grants and had all of my grades transferred from Widener University to Millersville University.

Just like that, I received the green light to continue my education. Mom gave me a car and I loaded it up and headed off to Amish country, Lancaster County, PA. Millersville University was like most colleges and universities I had already visited or partied at, although it was 4 to 5 times larger than Wideners Delaware Campus. I stayed on campus in a co-ed dorm called Gage Hall.

From the start, I found myself struggling academically.

I had signed up for health education, sales management, organization theory, world environment, and computer logic. Boy was I out of my league! Consequently, I resorted once again to cheating, only this time even my best efforts came up short.

Eventually, I dropped health education and sales management. This helped out a little, but my world came to a crashing halt when one of my teachers told me she had no idea how I made it this far and wanted to know how I got into college. The harsh reality was that various ways of manipulation were the only reason I had made it through. My choices and life's events wired me this way. There I sat in front of my teacher who told me that I should not be in her class at all, and she was certain I was not going to pass unless I knew how to express myself and my thoughts in essay form.

Cut straight to the chase - I could not write a paragraph with correct sentence structure, spelling and grammar, let alone an essay. I agreed with her and there was no reason to continue with her class.

This led me to question why I was there at all, and abruptly I went where I felt accepted. I returned to Widener University's Delaware campus, not to continue my education, but to pick up where I left off in search of myself. I lived a foul life and the more I did, the more I wanted to do.

One day while I was back at Millersville visiting with one of my frat brothers and my girlfriend at the time, I found myself in rare form. The three of us had been tripping on magic mushrooms, drinking Yukon Jack with lime juice and who knows how many beers in between. What I recall before my minor black out was this: we were loud, laughing, and I was not ready to stop. A boy who lived across the hall did not like what was taking place so he knocked on our door asking us to please keep the noise down. What happened next, I believe, was my boy and I stepped into the hallway and jumped on this guy. The guy was caught off guard and after we lumped him up, we went back into my friend's room and continued being rowdy.

Later that week I was called into the dean's office and placed on probation (which is funny in itself since I wasn't even a registered student at the time!). I was upset and told the dean that this guy started the whole ordeal by saying racial slurs – a bold face lie on my part. The truth was I remembered very little about that night; however, the results of my actions were very clear - this guy's eyes were raccooned and his pride was crushed. He was a wrestler in very good shape and I am almost certain that if the fight had been one-on-one, he would have given me more than I could have handled and then some.

One day when I was on my way to the bathroom from my dorm room, he caught me alone in the hallway. All of sudden I felt this vibe that someone was walking up on me and when I turned around I knew what time it was. Instead of mixing it up with this guy who wanted a fair rematch, I simply used my wit to avoid the inevitable and walked up to him and said, "Don't do it unless you want more of the same." Then I kept it moving and went on about my business.

Not being in college, I knew that I needed a Plan B... you know, something productive. Hanging out on campus, drinking beer and chasing after tail was not going to do it for me or get me far in life. I needed an income, so I went back to work for Coca-Cola and signed on as a permanent employee. The supervisors appreciated my past performance as a merchandiser from the previous summer. I paid my union dues and was assigned as a temporary driver.

Earning a paycheck made me feel good and working hard paid off in my favor. One day the plant manager asked me to run a truckload of product out to one of the local supermarket chains. He explained my assignment and I went right to work. My drive and work ethic opened the door for me to get my own route. I was soon sent out on a run to the Plymouth Meeting, PA area to unload a truck of soda. While unloading, I spotted a supervisor who came out of nowhere. He walked up to me and told me to take a break, that he had something he wanted to share with me. He asked if I wanted my own route and, before I could think, the word "yes" blurted out of my mouth. He was pleased with my quick response.

At age 21, I landed my own route as a driver for a well-known Fortune 500 Company. I was on my way. The following day I picked up my new route, and even though it was not the cream of the crop, it was mine, and I would now receive a small percentage for every case I now sold off my truck.

While driving and delivering, I built relationships with everyone in the company, from co-workers to management. I was well liked and very open for help. Other drivers gave me pointers with unloading product, short cuts in my route and how to avoid traffic, plus how to sell extra cases of soda. I appreciated their insight and willingness to assist me. I really enjoyed the family atmosphere. My job with Coca-Cola was going great, that was until I saw an opportunity to take advantage of my own situation.

While working at an ACME store on my route, I slipped and fell. Normally this would not be a big deal and all I needed to do was get up and continue to work, but I chose to get over on the system. I claimed an injury to my left knee; however, the truth be told, there was nothing wrong with my knee – but there was something very wrong with my thinking. The ACME

Manager made a report. I fabricated the entire incident and rehashed what I thought to be an academy award-winning story. After filing the necessary paperwork for my claim, I went on leave and just like a broken record, I played the same old song over again.

June 1st, 1984…a day, not unlike any other day in my life that year, but one that will live in my memory as the start of bad choices that began my twenty-five plus years in and out of prisons. While coming home from a bar, I stopped at a local 7-11 store to order two hotdogs – still my 'calm down' food after drinking. I recognized the girl working behind the counter; she was someone I knew from high school. We began a relaxed, civil conversation. However, as soon as she turned her back to prepare my food, my blood-shot eyes spotted two stacks of Pennsylvania Lottery tickets, about 500 total.

Without a thought, I reached over the counter, grabbed them, and put them in the waistband of my pants. When she turned around, she was none the wiser and I paid for my hot dogs and left. Driving home I knew that within the tickets I was about to become a winner and all I needed to do was scratch the tickets to find out what I won.

Well, I was not home for more than 20 minutes when I saw car headlights coming up on our block. As I looked closer, they were not lights of a normal vehicle, but that of a police car. The cruiser stopped in front of the house and a police officer got out with a flashlight and began to look in my car. I needed to do something.

Not wanting the officer to bring all kinds of questions by ringing the bell and waking up my mom, I immediately went outside to meet him. The officer asked me if this was my car; I already knew why he was there so I offered to help. I retrieved the lottery tickets thinking all I needed to do was return them and I would go my merry way. Seriously, that was my logic at the time.

Well, my logic was dead wrong! I was loaded into the cop car and escorted to the Lansdale Police Department. I was certain the girl at the counter did not see me take the tickets; I found out later I was correct. It was her manager, who was in the walk-in cooler and saw my every move.

When I walked out of the store, he acted quickly and proceeded to write down my license plate number before I sped off. He asked the girl if she knew me, and of course, everybody knows Ronald James.

From the very beginning, I was up front with the police officer and surprisingly very honest - mainly because I wanted to go home, get to sleep, and forget all about this experience. However, me going home was not on the officer's agenda, and I was caught off guard by his demeanor.

This guy was so nice when he met me on my mom's lawn, when he was asking me questions, and when pulled out his little card and read me my rights. He told me from the start that we would take a trip down to the station so I could answer a few questions. "Trust me", he said, "it is not a big deal and you will be back home in no time."

However, when we got to the station and sat down at his desk, there was a complete transformation of him. He became aggressive, lashing out with his tongue and an onslaught of venomous questions that left me in a daze. He played both roles of Dr. Jekyll and Mr. Hyde very well; his game was outstanding! Talk about the good cop, bad cop routine! Each question was very pointed and used to weaken my credibility.

As we moved further into the booking process, his questions became deadlier than the ones before. I felt helpless, giving in, and spilling my guts to the truth of what had happened. Yes, I told on myself. I realized that this was not stickball, organized tee-ball for kids, or even little league. This was the big league, the major play, and I was right in the middle of it.

All of this was made very clear to me after spending an hour with this officer answering his questions. Then to make matters worse, I had to have my photo taken at various angles, finger printed, and then locked in a cage like a wild animal without the comforts of home. What the hell just happened? Why was I in this predicament? How can I get out of here? Did the police believe what I said? Will I go to jail? Hey, don't I get a phone call?

As I sat there in that holding tank, these questions and hundreds of others raced through my mind for what seemed like hours. I began to beat myself up with the should've, would've, could've. Truth be told, deep inside of my being, I was feeling lonely, scared, humiliated and tired, but none of the feelings swirling around inside me were strong enough to get me to change or stop what I was doing.

Why I did not choose to hate this lifestyle, just like I chose to hate reading? It would have been so easy for me if I could have associated these feelings of shame, rejection and feeling insignificant when getting caught with that experience in order to change the course of my life. All I had to do was stop, just like I did when the children laughed at me in front of my fourth grade class. I would have shut the book of that lifestyle and slammed it down, never to revisit it again. Why? I would have told myself I hated going to jail, I hated all those questions, I hated being told what to do, not having control, being taken advantage of by others. I hated this lifestyle and my way of thinking, but the reality of this situation was I liked pleasing myself more than I hated any of those things.

As a matter of fact, I loved it because it was like a game of cat and mouse. I received all kinds of attention and, for some reason, I enjoyed the challenge of coming back after being down and out.

I went before a district judge who presented me with more questions and then set my bail. I was released on my own recognizance by the magistrate, but not before a lecture of encouragement to get me to put my life in order. Well, I hit the jackpot with those lottery tickets after all.

On August 6, 1984, I went before Judge Yong in the Montgomery County Courthouse in Norristown, PA and was sentenced to two years of probation. Yes, another slap on the wrist! Again, my life seemed to recycle itself. My focus remained in hot pursuit of serving myself.

I was out of work and my only source of income was my bi-weekly workman's compensation check, and to top it off, I was now on probation. This made me very depressed and I looked for gratification to fulfill my personal desires on a daily basis. I suffered from an acute case of 'poor me' syndrome and, even after these recent experiences, I still had no vision, no direction and no real cash flow.

I moved on with what I thought was a brilliant idea and one that would take care of the 'poor me' I was feeling. My cousin, Marvin, had just come home from the state penitentiary (the penn). I looked up to him, so what he said made sense to me in achieving a better lifestyle…so we began to sell drugs.

The good news is the moment you decide what you know is more important than what you have been taught to believe, you have shifted gears in your quest for abundance. Success comes from within, not from without.

-Ralph Waldo Emerson

CHOICE THREE
ME, MYSELF and I

MARVIN HAD SPENT HIS time in Graterford State Prison because he was busted for selling meth to an undercover cop in Montgomery County, Pa. When I met with Marvin, he shared a strong message - preaching restoration, family first, independent capitalism - and then he elaborated on building an empire for our family to enjoy. He made it clear that our position was to get the family back to its original financial state.

Marvin was a type of Moses in my eyes, leading us to the Promised Land. Yes, a land filled with milk and honey… more like millions and honey. He felt we should pick up where other family members had failed, and where his older brother Tyrone left off.

My cousin, Tyrone Palmer, was a multi-millionaire drug kingpin. He operated the business with street smarts and grace; however, Ty's life was cut short. He was gunned down and killed on Easter Sunday in Atlantic City, April 2, 1972 in a nightclub then known as Club Harlem. There have been a number of speculations, theories, and even books as to why Mr. Millionaire, Fat Daddy or Fat Tyrone Palmer was murdered. I chose to trust a source that revealed information I believed was closer to the truth about what went down.

Early in 1972, Frank Matthews, who was a drug lord from New York City, sent a large consignment of drugs said to be worth $250,000 to Philadelphia. This consignment was to be split with Richard "PI" Smith of South Philly. However, PI's greed got the best of him and he wanted the full consignment for free. He made contact with the Black Mafia to protect him in the event any problems would arise, and this protection was said to be at a cost of about $50,000.

The consignment was sent to Philly and delivered to PI; however, he claimed it was never received. He stated Tyrone must have taken it. In the meantime, Frank Matthews never received his payment for the package. He jumped on an Amtrak train to Philadelphia to locate the problem. Upon his arrival and meeting with PI, he questioned him about his money and the drugs. PI told Frank that Tyrone had intercepted the package. After the meeting, Frank left and traveled to North Philly to speak with Tyrone. During the meeting, Tyrone claimed that PI did receive the package, but Frank was not up for games.

Tyrone felt a certain way about being labeled unreliable and a thief, so he simply pulled out a briefcase with an untold amount of cash and said to Frank, "If you believe I stole anything from you, then take this case full of cash." Frank was satisfied that Tyrone was not the issue.

Later on, Frank fixed the problem and PI was found dead in a section of Philly called 'the Bottom'. This upset those associated with the Black Mafia who were still seeking payment from PI. A group called Black Inc., namely Sam Christian, now demanded payment from Tyrone, who refused to pay. I tell this event only because I often wonder what would have become of Tyrone if he was never killed, and who I would have become if Tyrone had lived to influence me.

Now I was on a quest to regain our family's title. The plan was simple - we needed a package. Marvin wanted to flood the streets of Philadelphia with coke and dope. After this task was completed, we could move into other areas. I was told all about his connections, his trusted workers, and his no-nonsense policy to anyone who would dare cross us. I replayed his words repeatedly in my head; they were music to my ears.

For the first time in my life, I could see everything he talked about. I was about to do something I felt I was meant to do. I was wide open and sold on this dream of no more money problems. Ironically, in the beginning, the problem was we needed cold hard cash to put the plan into motion. My brain moved into action and I was able to secure a loan for a thousand dollars and second for two thousand dollars.

Part One of the plan had us on a very enjoyable cross-continental flight. Marvin and I landed in Los Angeles mid-day, excited about getting the next phase of our plan underway. We immediately picked up our luggage and checked into one of the airport hotels. Marvin made the phone call to his contact, assuming his connection was going to meet us at the hotel, but to our surprise, we were invited to stay at the contact's condo in Santa Ana, Orange County, California.

The problem was that he would not be able to pick us up until later that night, so Marvin told him we would catch a cab. The ride seemed to take hours, although I certainly did not mind because the view was exciting. I saw a lot of sports cars, women, palm trees, miles of large interstate highways and lots of sun. The warm west coast breeze was blowing in my face from the open cab window. It reminded me of all the good times I spent as a youth traveling with my dad in the back seat of his car.

When we reached our destination, I was totally impressed by what I saw in this 2-bedroom plush condo. We were buzzed in with the contact's security system that linked cameras to the TV in the condo, so he saw us the moment we pulled up. Marvin's contact stood about six foot two inches tall and was well built. He was brown skinned and in his early forties. His conversation was rock solid and he ran down everything that Marvin and I wanted to hear. He covered all the bases, especially when he spoke of all of us becoming filthy rich and that we could buy as much product as we wanted from him.

Marvin negotiated a deal. We gave him the cash and he told us, he would sit on the coke and give us the product right before we began our travel back to the east coast. He said there was no need for us to have coke on our person; this was to protect us in case something went down. We were ok with that arrangement because I would be responsible for carrying the "Girl" (coke) back to Philly.

With several days before our flight heading back, I could rest at ease. The contact bragged about the quality of the "Girl" by telling us she could stand a three, "Meaning you could mix or cut it with other products to increase your profits." He wanted us to know, even with that mixture, we stood to have better coke than anyone else in Philly.

Marvin was on point, he did not drink alcohol, mess with drugs or smoke. I resorted to drinking beers and moving along as planned. I felt good about being in the business of selling drugs; however, my mood was broken when a big black brother, who stood an even six foot, weighing in at a whopping 300 pounds, appeared out of one of the rooms. He had a salt and pepper afro with a long, unmanaged beard.

My body tensed up expecting the worst from the abrupt intrusion as I glanced at Marvin. I could see he was calm and in control, but I watched his eyes and could tell he was calculating the situation without missing a beat. The contact introduced his muscle as the trouble shooter, who went by the name "Bear". He was true to the name and it fit him well. He was from Topeka, Kansas and when he opened his mouth, he sounded as country as Larry the Cable Guy, you know…'Git-R-Done'. After talking with him for a few hours, I realized he was an all right brother and I appreciated our company together.

Marvin and I were enjoying our down time and decided to fall back and crash in the living room as our temporary living quarters. Worn out from the flight from Philadelphia to LA, the road trip from LA to Santa Ana, and all the excitement of dreaming about becoming a millionaire put me right out. We woke up late the following day and all I could think about was getting something to eat. My tank was empty and Marvin's sentiments were definitely in line with mine, so we jumped up, washed, got dressed in our east coast gear, and were ready for action.

I took the liberty of scouting out the refrigerator and noticed something very wrong with the picture. There was no food, only water and a few beers. The contact seemed to have it going on, but I thought that all players kept food on hand. I shrugged it off and counted the empty fridge as him being too busy to stop by the market. My thoughts were kind. I have heard it said, "What is done in the dark will soon show its ugly face in the light."

Things certainly began to change and quickly. I watched the pendulum slowly sway back, from right to wrong, and then totally out of order. It blew our minds as we began to see what we were dealing with, noticing Bear and the contact could not be found. We thought they must have been out, taking care of business California-style. Unfortunately, we did not know how to disarm the security system and felt trapped, even though we were hungry and wanted to head out for a bite to eat … so we sat and watched TV.

When the contact finally returned, Marvin said, "Hey Jim, we are heading out to get something to eat." The contact offered to drive us, but we turned him down because we wanted to stretch our legs and check out the sights. After a good sit down meal, we viewed the area, took some pictures and then headed back to the condo.

After we settled in for the evening, we noticed the contact became distant. He stayed in his room for hours at a time, only to show his face for a moment, asking if we were we all right then slipped out of sight again. Bear rarely came out of the room and I began to wonder if these guys were gay?

The following morning was a beautiful sunny day in California, so Marvin and I headed to the pool and Jacuzzi. I sat back soaking up the sun while dreaming about buying real estate, like this condo …Yes! I knew how I was going to spend my first million.

My dreams were interrupted when we got back inside. Bear and the contact continued to act strange in their movements. When they appeared, they were methodical and weary. At this point, Marvin and I looked at each other, wondering what in the world was going on. We noticed crazy things happening with the contact – he looked as if he saw a ghost, his eyes were the size of half dollars, and beads of sweat dripped profusely from his brow. Marvin watched like a hawk his every move. The contact slowly walked over to the living room coffee table, picked up the TV remote, and flicked through the channels. He stopped when he reached the security channel with the surveillance on the front door.

Wearing only a pair of pants, standing bare-chest and

barefoot, his chest was expanding and contracting as if he just ran a 100-meter dash from the police. I looked closer and could see his heart pounding strongly, as if it would jump clear out of his chest. I knew something was wrong, but what? Marvin knew something was wrong – I could see it in his eyes. Would there be an ambush on the condo? Could it be stickup men, the feds, or someone who had some beef with these guys? I felt like we were in the wrong place at the wrong time and we were trapped.

As the contact approached the kitchen, I looked at Marvin to try to anticipate his next move. Marvin eased out of his chair and walked slowly toward the contact. Before Marvin could speak, he was shut down and told to be quiet, so I moved in to investigate.

I was unable to determine what would happen next based on the tone of the contacts voice, but I knew I was not going to let anything go down without a fight. There we were…three peas in a pod huddled close in the kitchen. We remained completely still…until the contact motioned for us to get down. As he dropped to the floor first, we quickly followed.

Whatever was going down, it was serious. The contact slowly placed his index finger against his lips, motioning us to remain still and quiet. There was fear written all over his face. I felt helpless and clueless to what would happen next.

Crouched on the floor, I began to determine my next move. My eyes focused on the contact as he began to stare at the ceiling. Next, he pointed at us, then to the ceiling. Desperately I tried to locate what he wanted us to see…surely something had this guy spooked. I noticed an object protruding from the ceiling; it resembled a portion of metal you would see connected to a fire sprinkler system. He slowly leaned over, pulling us together and whispered in a childlike voice, "They are listening to us."

Okay, when I heard this, the first question I was thinking, "Who the hell is he talking about? What the hell am I doing on this kitchen floor...wait a minute, why the hell am I here again?" Was this really the drug lifestyle that I wanted so badly to be part of? There was a resounding press for me to look deeper, way beyond this current situation, to address the defining question of why I was there. What was or what is my purpose in life? I am supposed to be a major drug dealer with money, women, power and wealth...following those in my family who made it big. Why then am I on this kitchen floor?

Maybe there was to be something more out of life because so far, I was finding that selling drugs seemed loopy. After twenty minutes of theatrics, the contact jumped up as if nothing happened and simply walked out of the kitchen. He looked back and asked if we were all right, as he disappeared into his bedroom.

What kind of question is that, were we all right? HELL NO! I have never seen anything like that in my life! To make matters worse, Bear emerged looking like a big zombie making no responses even when spoken to; he stared right through us. He walked around the condo for a few minutes then returned to his room.

About an hour later the contact returned with the same textbook scene as if he done this a thousand times before. This time, though, there was a major difference. Marvin had a scowl on his face and made it clear we were not going through that same experience again! He told the contact we were not going to the kitchen, not getting on the floor, nor were we going to be quiet. As a matter of fact, we began to laugh out loud and mimicked the contact. Marvin informed him the gig was up. He explained they did not have to continue doing things in private, what was done in the dark finally came to light. They were smoking coke, free-basing, to be exact!

Now that everything was out in the open, the contact began to take his equipment and lay it out. He was the first person I ever saw put a bricker brack pipe to his lips – better known as "sucking the glass dick". I wondered why anyone would spend hours of valuable time placing a glass instrument in his or her mouth instead of counting the money.

They burned up coke, literally setting it on fire, and watched their cash go up in smoke. I, for the life of me, could not understand why anyone would do something as idiotic as this, but this was how Marvin and I were going to make our millions…off idiots.

Just for the record, my eventual curiosity on the matter ended up killing all but one of my nine lives.

The following day, the contact made his move and we had the coke in our possession. Finally, it was time to leave; however, we had the small problem of escorting the 'girl' on the flight. It was my job to transport her home, so I placed her in my carry-on case. On the way to the airport, all that remained in my thoughts was, "please don't let me get jammed up." I do not remember if this petition was to God or myself; all I knew was I did not want to go to jail. We landed in Philadelphia Airport safe and sound, YES!

Being a so called 'official drug dealer' did not help my situation, why… because I became an official user, too. I began using coke with both friends and family, and, even though my drug use was light, it was none-the-less drug use. I took a trip from Philly to New Jersey to see a friend who wanted an eight ball of the 'girl'. This was something light – just to put a few dollars in my pocket – so I went to Marvin and he bagged it up for me.

With the coke in tow and tired from the hustle and bustle of the streets of Philly, I finally made the 2-hour drive back to North Jersey to my place at the YMCA in Montclair. I was renting this room on a weekly basis so that I could be close to my girlfriend at the time. After I arrived and settled down from the trip, I thought a short nap would be in order before I met up with my boy and girlfriend.

I sat back on the small bed and analyzed my situation and, for the first time, noticed the dimensions of the room. It was no bigger in area than an 8 x 12 foot size walk-in closet. The lighting was dim with an eerie presence that overshadowed me.

After I collected my thoughts, I stood up, emptied my pockets, and placed everything on the table next to the bed. The baggie containing the coke caught my eye and I focused in on the white powder. Then I heard a voice…the voice I had not heard in a long time, but certainly not the voice I needed to hear.

I was not sure where the voice was coming from – elsewhere in the room or from the coke in the bag. What I was sure of was that the voice spoke clearly and I heard its cry…more like a yearning for me to pick it up. I felt moved to follow its lead. I thought to myself that one small line could not hurt. Hell, my boy would not even miss a small crumb now, would he?

Therefore, I began to sort through the baggie of coke looking to pull out a small chunk of the white substance. When I found what I was looking for, I placed it on a crisp one-dollar bill that I had creased down the middle lengthwise.

Then I crunched and crushed the coke between the dollar bill until it was a fine powder.

While I was performing this process of crushing the coke and without even realizing, my body went through some sort of change. My heart began beating excessively fast, I became somewhat winded, and my hands started to sweat and shake. I took a deep breath and was able to get myself together enough to continue the process. It had to be from the excitement, the anticipation, the feeling of doing something wrong that felt so right. I rolled up an additional dollar bill to serve as a scoop. It was time to serve myself.

I took my dollar scooper, picked up a small portion of the white stuff, and sniffed the product until it was gone from the bill. I then placed my finger against my left nostril, placed a little water in my nose, and tilted my head back to clear the nose cavity.

As usual, I received the instant gratification that came with this high – the tingling sensation in my brain, followed by the numbness and then the drip at the back of my throat. I then began a conversation with myself and I said, "Self…" and myself said, "Hmmm?" I said, "Let's snort some more coke right now." Myself said, "Man, let's get to moving playa, gotta go get that dollar from your boy." I stood up and said, "I am feeling reeaal good right now 'cause I am in heaven and there ain't no need to rush this." As I was finishing the crushed coke left in the bill, I realized an hour had passed during my madness. Time flies when you are having fun…and having a three-way conversation with yourself!

After a lengthy conversation between Me, Myself and I about taking the remainder of the coke to my boy and collecting his cash, I convinced the 'Me' and 'Myself' characters to do something to get motivated, so I opened the package again and dumped a nice sized portion on the bill. The more I snorted, the more it felt like my mind was racing. All of my thoughts were preoccupied, hearing every sound and every movement. It seemed as if my hearing was bionic; it was so intensified that I could hear people down the hall in other rooms, outside and in my head.

This went on for hours and hours. Needless to say, sometime the next morning I had completely snorted the rest of that package. The eight ball was gone and now I was faced with breaking the news to both my boy and Marvin. My friend was easy – I simply told him I could not get my hands on anything. Marvin, on the other hand, was another story. He was looking for cold hard cash. How was I going to explain my usage?

I sat on the edge of the bed, all my thoughts consumed with coming up with a believable story that I could sell to Marvin. With both hands holding my head, my elbows resting on my knees, and my brain in overdrive I thought to myself, "Fine mess you have gotten yourself into!" No sooner than I allowed this thought to rest in my brain that I came up with a solution. I ran it through my CPU a few times, making sure it was foolproof. Once I realized it was a winner, I ran downstairs to the telephone located in the YMCA lobby. I called Marvin and this is what I said, "Hey Cuz, guess what, you are never gonna believe this. When I met with my boy late last night to drop off his candy, he dumped it out on a plate and sat it on the card table where we were sitting. As I got up to go to the kitchen to get a beer, I knocked over the table, spilling the drinks and the candy on his shag carpet. I did my best to help him pick up what I could, which did not amount to much. I spoiled his night and counted it as a loss. I am so sorry Cuz."

I waited for an answer and when it came, there was no

sign of disappointment, anger or hesitation in his voice. Marvin simply said, "No problem, we don't sweat the crumbs." With that weight of guilt off my shoulders, I was able to go back upstairs and crash for a few hours. I still wanted to serve myself by meeting up with my girlfriend, and when the time came to meet Marvin, we continued business as usual.

We moved all around the city making drops and collecting cash from a number of his workers; however, we ran into the same old problems. Either we spent our cash as fast as we got it, or it seemed as though everyone had an excuse not to pay and some of the excuses were lamer than others. With no real plan for my future, other than being a major drug dealer, I was in dire need of cold hard cash. Somehow, I needed to figure out how to get out of this situation and get my hands on some funds; the drug game was not for me.

I spotted an ad in the newspaper for a sales position. This job seemed to be right up my alley. Their office was close enough in Fort Washington, PA, and the position promised you could make as much money as you wanted – the sky was the limit. I got on the phone and dialed the number listed in the ad; I was excited and my heart raced with anticipation. The phone rang a few times before someone answered, "Thank you for calling Successful Singles International (SSI) How may I help you?" I told the receptionist I was calling about the sales position advertised in the local paper. She provided me with the office information and told me to come in and fill out an application.

When I arrived at the office and walked through the front door, I was blown away and knew this place was for me. The office was buzzing with excitement, phones were jumping off the hook, and there were people walking around professionally dressed. Others were running back and forth to accomplish various tasks and everyone wore a smile. Those who were in charge gave the impression that they were God's gift to the world. I loved it! Even their furniture was high end. The entire office atmosphere carried the aura of success.

My head spun in every direction trying to observe it all and I was sold! Then I was called into one of the manager's offices. The manager was from Egypt; the guy was immaculate and his interview approach was flawless. I sold myself to him by telling him just how important this job was to me. The truth of the matter was any job was important to me at this stage of the game only because I was unemployed and broke. I was told to come back for a second interview the following week.

When Monday came around, I was there early with my game face on. I was ushered into his office by a beautiful secretary. Any other time I would have tried to put my mac down on her, but at this point, she did not have what I needed. As I sat down, the office door closed and the manager began immediately to tell me, "Mr. James, I do not believe you are cut out for this line of work." Was this guy some kind of nut or was he plum crazy? Why would he have me come all the way to his office to tell me that?

Immediately, I went into my defense mode. I started by overcoming that objection and every other objection he threw at me. He sat back in his high priced leather chair and listened...I then became animated and sold myself. He then stood up, smiled and shook my hand, congratulating me. I had passed the test. However, when he said, "Mr. James, you have the job!" I was still on guard ready to give another comeback statement.

He went on to explain their company uses a technique called the 'take away approach' to interviewing. This was done to see if I really wanted the job and then he added that

I should fit right in. I was informed my training would begin that week and he expected to see me there on time. I spent three days in training before I was sent out on my first run with one of the assistant managers. I did not get the sale, but I knew I could handle the work. It took me a few runs to get into the grove, but once I found it, it was game on!

SSI was simply a high class dating service. I enjoyed meeting people and was able to network with various professionals, business owners, state workers, prison guards, computer geeks, nurses, doctors and high-class models. Those with money, all the way down to the average Joe, who was hard up to find love. It was a common practice to begin all of my interviews with a full financial profile. There was no need to proceed if that person could not afford our services.

I retrieved clients vital statistics, which involved gathering their personal information, bank and credit card information along with numbers, background reporting and signatures. It was a lot of work that seemed pointless; however, it was needed and important in order to gauge their financial stability and help to qualify them for membership.

Finally…I was doing big things and felt good about myself, but after one hundred or so interviews, I started to run into a wall. I was informed this type of thing happens to even the best of sales people, so I left SSI to do the only other thing that made sense…drug dealing. Really?! That makes sense?!…well it did at the time.

Marvin and I traveled to the Logan section of the city and hooked up with a friend of his who was now our new contact; only he was not getting high like our friend in California. This guy was about the dollar and his product was good and at a great price. We grabbed what we needed and moved forward. The plan was simple. Marvin would conduct business as usual in Philly, while allowing me to explore some new business opportunities out of state.

My old frat brother and I were to transport some of the white stuff across state lines to Marvin's younger brother, Peanut, who lived in the mid-west part of Kansas. Peanut quoted some prices to us, which were twice as high as what we sold "the girl" for, so we stood to make a killing. Road trip to Kansas, here we come! My boy and I packed, gassed up, put expense and toll money in our pockets, and the triple beam and the girl in the back seat.

After many miles, we reached Wichita, Kansas where we spent three to four weeks in the night life, hard core partying and sleeping with all types of women. We were just about to break even, but there was one other thing to do before leaving the area. We met up with Peanut at a local gun shop in order to purchase a .38 caliber revolver and shells for Marvin. We loaded the car with our things, the triple beam and whatever cash we had left, along with the gun. Like the tornado we came in on, we were out of that town and heading home.

Back in Philly, Marvin and I started to struggle more and more. We both blew money just as fast as it came in. The cash was never reinvested in the product. Instead, we used it to put out family fires like rent, bills and whatever else came up, including our needs. The dream of being a multi-millionaire drug dealer like Marvin's late cousin, Tyrone, was not happening. It seemed as if there was a curse on us. I started to take some things into my own hands. I felt that my recent drug-dealing course went very well in Kansas and, even if I messed up a few dollars here and there, I was always somehow able to recover.

It was the heart of the summer of 1985 and crack cocaine had just exploded onto the streets of Philadelphia. Cocaine

- whether soft (powder) or hard (crack) - was a viable, vibrant business. Coke was in almost every area of every section of the city and being sold on the open street corners. If someone wanted to get rich, they claimed a corner and went to work. It was as if those who sold coke had a legal license to do so. Lines accumulated from its great demand. People stood toe to toe up and down the street, alongside houses, in and out of alleyways and around corners waiting for the white stuff. Sometimes the lines were so backed up it was as if they were standing at a checkout counter in a local Wal-Mart Super Store.

There was a sense of pride, honor and integrity with many families who ran the "true corners". There were around-the-clock workers who ran shifts, with sales men and women who sold hand to hand. There were also people who bagged up their product, those who supervised crowd control, and those who looked out for new customers, robbers and police.

God forbid you were discovered to be one of the robbers. If so, and they did not beat you half to death or kill you, you had a neighborhood full of people, including grandmothers and children, chasing you down. The corners brought in hundreds of thousands of dollars daily and no one monkey was going to stop their show.

That included someone else selling anything on his or her corners. If you dared to cut in on their action, there were maximum consequences. It could cost a person his or her life. There were drugs sold at every opportunity all across the city - from the projects to make shift storefronts, individual houses, abandoned houses, and even cars. It seemed to be an open marketplace.

Out of all the spots the drug was sold, there was nothing like the corners of 8th and Butler, 9th and Pike, 8th and InPrincess

D, and 5th and Glenwood. This was an all-together different culture. Together they all spoke in a different language and, if you were not on the top of your game, you had no business being in the area. It was as if you landed in a foreign country with adversaries on all sides and, for the most part, you were surrounded.

The streets were run predominately by Puerto Ricans. If you were not down with their codes, you were on your own. Words like 'agua', which means 'water' in Spanish, but on the streets, it was interpreted as "Get your ass off the corner because the police are coming!" It was crazy how hundreds of people could literally vanish in the blink of an eye. Those who were out to purchase the white stuff learned quickly how to get out of the way during times like these.

On the other hand, a few choice words were music to their ears. When you heard BLUE, YELLOW or RED TAPE, or BLACK, BLUE or STAR BAGS, it referred to those families who sold the coke and who were advertising their supply for sale. Literally, everyone had his or her hand in on the action in one form or another…everyone except my cousin Marvin and yours truly!   Others were flourishing, but we struggled to keep things afloat in our own operation, and then a major problem occurred. Someone made the mistake of pushing the envelope too far in Marvin's direction concerning disrespect. Marvin was not having it. He called me aside and as we spoke, I knew right from the get-go something was terribly wrong. There was an absolute change in his demeanor, having the look of death on his face. His eyes were fire red, voice low and not clear at all, which was very different from the upbeat person I knew and was with on a daily basis. It was as if he was somewhat winded, however, he was very calm and in control.

The first thing he told me was he might have to kill

someone today…okay, there was no doubt that what he said was 100% factual. He only needed to know was I able to assist him. There was no question in my mind I was all in, ready to defend my family, even if it meant to the death. How could I not be in on this? Marvin was my brother.

He sat me down and went over his plan. He wanted me to carry the loaded .38 that we brought back from Kansas. We would be heading out to an apartment in East Germantown; Marvin wanted to drive. I was totally fine with the decision because my hands were already full. I got ready by physically preparing myself, which involved slamming down a beer, putting on my green army jacket, and placing the cold steel pistol into my right jacket pocket. I felt just like Robert Deniro in the movie *The Taxi Driver*. Was I ready…Damn straight! Was I nervous…Damn straight!! But this was Marvin we were talking about, so I had to pull myself together.

It is a wonder I did not shoot myself because I never took my finger off the trigger. All Marvin wanted me to do was hand him the gun at the appropriate time and he would handle his business from there. As we parked the car down the street from the apartment building, my mind started to flow with all kinds of questions like, 'If Marvin got hurt, what would I do? What if someone else got hurt? What if something happened to me? What if the cops come?'

I knew this was not the time for me to ask a lot of questions, no way! This was not a game and Marvin made that very clear to me before we left the car. He paused for a few seconds and then he sat back and braced his arms and hands on the steering wheel…maybe it was to check in and make peace with the Creator, but whatever the case, it was game on.

With a deep breath followed by a sigh, we were out. He told me that as soon as we got to the door of the guy's apartment, hand him the gun. He was going to knock on the door and handle whatever came down the pike.

The scene was perfect for a homicide – there was absolutely no one in an eyes shot view from where I was standing. I knew that the sound of gunfire would draw a crowd...so we only had a few seconds to make this happen without giving ourselves away. Something was about to give.

Marvin placed his ear slowly towards the apartment door and I could tell by the look on his face he was pleased that our trip across town was not in vain. He stuck his hand out reaching in my direction and that was my queue. As I passed him the piece of steel, I knew this was it. It was about to go down. For many reasons, I felt powerless. When the gun was in my possession, there was a sense of authority affixed to my being, but when I passed it off, I felt empty...but I knew Marvin was in control.

My eyes were locked completely on him and I noticed he was in a strategic zone. The gun was now exposed, down by his side, and his movements were that of a completely different person, as I watched him ease very slowly into position. He tapped on the apartment door three times in quick repetitions. The next series of events that took place changed my thinking forever.

The door sprung open and the unsuspected victim's face turned white as a ghost. Instantly, the man began to plea for mercy, going straight for a bargaining agreement. It was as if he completed his final rehearsal and now was on stage for a Broadway show titled "This Is Your Life". He apologized for the rip, explaining he had no idea who Marvin really was. Someone with better sense must have pulled his coat.

Anyway, Marvin eased the pistol into his pocket without this guy ever seeing the gun, or how close to death he really was. I knew then that it was all right to fall back and humble myself in any situation, especially those that concern my life. I also realized that my cousin was not a heartless, cold-blooded killer who was out to gun down anyone for no apparent reason.

The rules of the streets may have dictated another outcome, but that day it was a win/win situation. No matter how bad things got with the drug selling career, neither Marvin nor I were willing to throw in the towel and call it quits.

Marvin wanted to visit one of his boys who had also recently gotten out of the penn. We drove up to the Logan section of the city. Up until this point, I had seen all types of homes throughout the city of Philadelphia - from the ghettos to apartment projects, spanning from North to South Philly, northeast to west. I was accustomed to going in and out of the shooting galleries, crack houses and "abandominiums" (boarded up city properties). I saw all kinds of filth, dirt, rats, roaches and paraphernalia from drug users. I met many people from all walks of life, and nothing seemed to surprise or shake me up, except being introduced to a man named George Diggs.

George lived on the second floor of a duplex apartment that he and his wife owned. As the three of us sat in his kitchen, Marvin and Diggs kicked the bobo talking about the who's who of prison life. I took notice to my surroundings and figured this guy's spot was a crack house. There were dishes stacked up in the sink, roaches running rampant, trash bags sitting in the corners so full they were ready to tip over, and an array of empty colorful coke bags on the table and in the ashtrays.

For me, none of this was out of the norm and pretty much how I lived some days; however, what was out of the norm was what I heard when this guy opened his mouth. I was flabbergasted with his dictionary. Outside of his slur, I realized George was extremely smart, so now he had my attention and I focused on their conversation. I was spellbound for almost a complete hour. This light skinned, heavy build brother with naturally black wavy hair stood about six foot tall, with a head the size of a large pumpkin …but that is not what had me spellbound for almost an hour! George was more than just smart…he was an intellectual genius and I was in a trance listening to his every word!

George Diggs was proficient in math, history, world events and the streets. Hands down he was a master at banking, business, criminal law and manipulation. What in the world was wrong with this picture though? Why was George Diggs sitting in the middle of a crack house in such filth? What happened? Why was he here and not out making millions of dollars at a top law firm or a CEO on Wall Street?

So my curiosity got the best of me and I jumped into the conversation to learn more. He came from good stock; he also had a very free spirit and took nothing to heart. All he wanted to do was make people smile. Once he engaged in deep conversation, every part of his body began to move. His thighs clapped together like a pair of garden shears. His hands were all over the place – in the air, on his head, his legs, the table, on me and Marvin's arm, the chair and then they were back on me again. Yet his hands, legs and feet had nothing on his gift of gab.

His mouth was gold and he certainly could talk…not to mention being creative, witty and funny. If you were out to get something from him, he would turn your selfishness against you and use it to his advantage, and if all else failed, he would use his snaggletooth, boyish smile to win you over. His words captured me as he went from sales pitch to closing the deal.

George explained to Marvin he was looking for a "friendly package", or someone who willingly turned over his or her ID and checkbook. If he could get his hands on the friendly package, getting our hands on the money would not be a problem. George was big time into checks and credit cards, explaining this is the way we needed to go. I thought to myself, who in their right mind would be willing to give up their personal ID and checkbook? Maybe this guy was crazy after all!

Moreover, I knew that messing with someone else's identity was dead wrong, but he went on to tell us that he could set up a fictitious corporation with tax ID numbers, bank accounts, and then he would take out loans and build credit... only to turn around and tear it down for cash. Once George got his hands on the money, he was off to the races.

I admired his ability to be open and forthright about his lifestyle and who he was. He claimed to live a very simple life. All he wanted was a dime bag of coke that he could either shoot up or smoke, some pussy to eat, a pack of Winstons, a Pepsi, and a 3-Musketeers candy bar for dessert.

Well, the seed was planted and he said if we wanted to get a few thousand dollars very quickly, all we had to do was come up with a friendly package. Then he named the specifics – checkbooks, MAC cards, credit cards, driver's license, social security cards, work ID, birth certificates, library cards or any form of ID. His words left a lasting impression as Marvin and I made our exit. Oh, but before we got out of the door, George made sure he hit us up for a twenty-dollar spot. That was his consultation fee, that would pay for his needs for that day, all except for the female company, which was why he had his wife.

For the most part, I enjoyed having fun with Marvin and everyone we dealt with enjoyed having a good time with us. However, the pendulum found its way to the other end of the spectrum, with none other than George Diggs. I thought long and hard on what George was looking for. He wanted vital statistics on people, so I grabbed the 100 or so profiles I held onto when I worked for SSI and thought about taking them to George. I told Marvin maybe we could sell these to him. I was certain that he could do something with them. If we could get a few hundred dollars for them, I would be happy. From what I could see, it was just information on paper.

Marvin and I headed to George's spot. When we got there, he was clearly excited to see us and I could not wait until he opened his mouth. I so much enjoyed hearing him speak. When I presented the profiles to him, I could tell from his body language he was somewhat let down. He said that what he was looking for was someone he could coach - meaning the friendly package should be someone willing - someone who would tell the police that they lost their wallet and follow up with a police report. This would protect the owner of the friendly package and allow him or her to regain all their credentials.

Then George popped the question to me, wanting to know if I would be willing to give up my own ID for some cash? I never gave it much thought since my checking account was closed. I told him this and he began to move all his body parts – he was excited and explained that did not matter. He could still use my stuff. I quickly processed everything that was at hand and then looked at Marvin for the final nod. Well, it was official…I had just become the friendly package!

George said all I needed to do was drop everything off to him, make the call to the police and file the report. He said to give him one week and we would have cash in hand. Well, that was music to our ears.

The following day Marvin and I dropped off the friendly package, followed George's instructions and met with the police and explained everything. The report was made and now all we had to do was wait…and wait we did.

A week went by and during that time I imagined all the new items on the laundry list we ordered from George, one of which was the latest television to replace my skimpy 13-inch television. I could not wait to hook up with George again and collect our stuff – jewelry, electronics, new gear and whatever else he could get his hands on…but mainly the cash!

The day came when we knocked on Diggs' door and did not get an answer. We came back a second time that week and third time the following week, still with no answer. The only explanation we could come up with was George Diggs' burned us. Marvin was undone; I never saw him so upset. He always kept his cool, but he said that something was going to have to give and it was not going to be us.

So, the next day, bright and early, we were in Logan. This time we parked around the corner and only rang the buzzer once. We waited a few moments and heard someone come to the door. It was George's wife and when she asked who it was in her very low sweet voice, Marvin snapped. "Open the door", he barked. The door slowly opened and through the crack, which was just wide enough for us to see the fear in her eyes, we heard her sweet voice say, "Oh, hello Marvin. I have not seen George".

Marvin did not give her a chance to say anything else; he erupted erratically, "if George Diggs don't answer this door the following day, there will be problems for anyone who lives here". His message meant business and she could see that we were upset. As we walked away, Marvin assured me not to worry and that Diggs was going to pay.

As promised, we showed up the following day and there was no hiding around the corner – no, we were bold and parked in front of their place and proceeded by going up and ringing the bell. All the while, and all because of greed, I remained hopeful that George would be there. I knew a deal was a deal, so if nothing else and George could not come through, I wanted my stuff returned.

I heard someone coming down the steps from inside, the door swung wide open and there stood George in just a pair of shorts, wearing a big 'ole smile. As usual, he was very excited to see us…at least that was what he projected. After we stepped in, we walked upstairs to his kitchen and we all sat down at the table.

His place was just like I remembered a few weeks earlier – the only sign of change was the number of excuses that ran out of his face. I was very aware of his BS, represented by a lot of laughing aloud, so this part of his class was rudimentary. Marvin cut his conversation very short by telling Diggs he had better come up with our money and the stuff he promised us.

I noticed how George's body language changed as Marvin read him the riot act, which was no act. He stopped moving his legs and his hands were still. It was clear he heard and understood what Marvin meant. Suddenly, he responded as if he came up with a solution to his problem. His legs, arms, hands and feet jumped into high gear, along with his mouth. He said something that I came to understand as George's true self, his gospel. A saying he only used when he really wanted to convey his integrity, thus came the words of a Prophet saying, "Listen, listen right!" which meant whatever was said after those three words were gospel.

He told us that we needed to come by his apartment the following evening at eight o'clock. He had someone very special he wanted us to meet and that person was going to solve all our problems. Marvin and I both knew that the only problem was Diggs giving us what he owed us. He told us his cousin was in town and she would square up his debt. It did not make a difference who paid, as long as they paid us the following day.

Whatever the case, George's mouth bought him some time and we gave him a pass and left. I questioned Marvin about his thoughts on the whole thing and he remained optimistic. He said that George was always able to produce and his word was good as gold in the penn, but we both knew that things always changed once the 'girl' came on the scene.

She, the 'girl' or coke, was always going to be first. That damn cocaine had everyone's nose, veins and lungs wide open.

"We live in a universe in which there are laws, just as there is a law of gravity. If you fall off a building it doesn't matter if you're a good person or a bad person…you're going to hit the ground."

-Michael Bernard Beckwith

CHOICE FOUR
GYPSY

AFTER RUNNING AROUND WITH Marvin, I returned to Germantown Avenue where I was now living. I was worn out, so I sat back on the sofa, turned on my 13-inch television, and thought about the better days ahead. If I only knew what was about to transpire, but I had no idea.

The following day rolled around and it was time for us to meet this so-called mysterious wonder woman who was going to save the day. Yeah right, the real "Golden Girl". It is easy to put stock into someone else and make them sound good. All you do is cap them up and sooner or later everyone believes the lie, including the originator of it. So, for this chick to impress me, the proof had better be in the pudding.

Diggs had paraded around the room and preached that she was a living legend, boasting of all her accomplishments, saying that in comparison to her, he was a peon. In my eyes, what he was saying really did not mean much. His words were empty and I compared him as a peon next to everybody else - a no good shyster and all I knew was that he, she, them, or whoever had better have something when we showed up.

Payday. We rang Diggs' doorbell and he came barreling down the stairs yelling, "They're here! They're here!" He swung the front door open ushering us in as if we were late.

Man, what a difference a day makes! George was all decked out in new gear. A new sweat suit, new sneakers, his hair groomed and I believe his teeth were in. His excitement was off the chart. He practically dragged us upstairs as he rambled on about something I could hardly understand. All I heard were those same three words; "Listen, listen right, she's about to leave."

Apparently, we showed up just in time. When we walked in his kitchen, the place looked as if a cleaning/catering service had come and flipped that apartment. The place was spotless, fit for ghetto dignitaries. The only thing that was messy was a corner filled with empty bags, boxes and wrappings from all the food, clothing and electronics.

The place was set up like Christmas morning. There was the sound of people's voices in the front room, as I heard the sound of the oldies playing in the background; the atmosphere was festive. There were all kinds of alcohol on the kitchen table, along with plenty of food, and my guess was that all the excitement drove the roaches into hibernation because there were none in sight.

Marvin and I took our normal seat at the kitchen table and, if seeing was believing, something was definitely different. Before I could take it all in, I heard a female's voice summon for George. He yelled back from the kitchen so his voice would be heard over the music, "Cheryl come here, I want you to meet them."

From the rip, her grand entry demanded respect. She took control of the situation by chastising George by making it perfectly clear it was wrong for him to use her government name, which was Cheryl Diggs, in front of unknown guests. She cut him swiftly with her mouth and the only thing George did was drop his head like a little boy who was told by his mother to go to his room. She told him to never use her real handle around strangers and, in the same breath without missing a beat, she very casually introduced herself as Gypsy.

Hmmm… Gypsy… the Webster's Dictionary definition for the word is 'a member of a nomadic people, perhaps of Hindu origin, with dark skin and hair; Egyptian was once believed it to be their origin.' The Oxford version says, 'a member of a traveling people.' Gypsy was her name and what those dictionaries said was a small portion of her game.

There she stood, an Egyptian queen about 5'10" tall, her light complexion was sunshine radiant. She had a distinctive beauty mole on her cheek and was draped from head to toe in very costly clothing. She wore a colorful silk scarf that was knotted on the side of her head, loosely swayed gently over her shoulder, and then laid across her breast. She swerved and spun her body ohhhh so elegantly past us. She was very agile, yet bold and confident with every move. There was purpose and meaning with every move, every gesture she made.

First she offered us a drink. Marvin declined, but I accepted a soda. I said, "I'll have some gin and a splash of 7-up" and she gingerly corrected me by saying "Oh no, baby, that's not gin, it's vodka." Vodka was certainly not my choice of poison, so I declined. However, with her quick wit she questioned, "Oh, do you like gin?" Feeling the shame of making a mistake asking for gin when there was a clear label on the bottle that said vodka, I felt a need to come back with something humorous, "Yes", I blurted out, "It makes me horny." Everyone laughed and thus set the tone.

I did accept a can of beer and took a few sips to unwind, but I still felt anxious and wanted to get what I came for – my money and my stuff! Marvin took the lead and he told Gypsy he was not sure what role she played in all of this, but we were there solely to receive compensation for what George owed us – nothing more, nothing less.

Gypsy politely cut Marvin short and said she had no idea what was going on. All she knew was George wanted her to meet someone (meaning us) who may have some work she may be interested in, something that could aid in making her money.

The mastermind George Diggs apparently was playing both ends from the middle. I asked her what kind of work was she talking about and she chimed in "Profiles" ...profiles? Then it hit me, she wanted to see the SSI profiles that I originally brought to George. The one hundred-plus worthless pieces of paper would have gone into the trash if I remembered to clean out my car a few days earlier. However, I still had them so I ran down to the car and brought the profiles inside for Gypsy to investigate.

After handing her the stack, she ran through each one meticulously as if she were an auditor. She had a pair of old lady style reading glasses with strings attached so you do not lose them. When she was done with her review, she removed her glasses and said she needed to do a test run. If it was good, I had a quick five hundred dollars and we could do business with the rest.

I thought to myself, "not so fast Ms. Gypsy, your big headed cousin just stuck me and now here you come." I told her how I had been trusting and up front, yet all I received in return was nothing. I was not sure what kind of game George was playing, but it was not right. She left the room without a word or response...was something wrong? She returned as few seconds later with a brand new VCR still in the box (a four hundred dollar piece of equipment back in those days) and she said, "This is something towards what George owes you." Then she dug in her pocket like a dude and peeled off two hundred dollars in cash and gave it to me. Her harsh remark about the cash was that George will work off the rest, and then she turned to him and scolded him on his integrity, saying this was her token of good faith with us.

She told us that she was not about game, but a professional business woman who was all about the dollar. She made it clear that she was willing to die for her word and would kill dirt or anyone who stood in her way. She put her lady act on hold and went straight gangster. Marvin understood the language and the two of them hit it off.

Now that they spoke the same lingo, Marvin found out that Gypsy had known his late brother Tyrone very well. Plus, the longer the conversation went on, the more Marvin found out she knew a host of others. She had ties with people in north, south, and west Philly, as well as everywhere in between. She announced her affiliations with the Black Underground Movements and other organizations.

Gypsy's rap was much different from George's and the truth was that both of them were equally smart. She, however, kept a high standard about herself and did not suffer from a get-over mentality, nor was she about conning anyone. What she did, what she believed in, was her lifestyle. The woman appeared to be in her thirties, although I am sure she had seen and done a lot in her short life.

She continued to tell us more about herself, but it was not in a braggadocios manner. You could tell she spoke from the heart and her truth was genuine. She opened up to us because of her past friendship with Tyrone. Gypsy spoke about her dealings with those in the underworld. She had connections with Move members, those involved with Black Incorporated, the South Philly Mob both Blacks and the Italians, the Irish mob, and not to mention her ties from New York to California.

She knew those in the entertainment lifestyle, and if you had any connection to Philadelphia and the circle town where everybody knew somebody, then you probably knew or heard of her, too. Gypsy's name rang bells, and yes, to me she appeared to be the real deal. Maybe she was this living legend that George boasted about after all.

I later found out she was the legend and the reason why was that her resume consisted of a rap sheet of jail time from county to the feds. In addition, she was a boss, so whatever she got her hands involved in, she ended up perfecting it, running it, and/or partnering with those who had anything to do with it. She went on to explain that she was a networking queen, able to get her hands on anything from anyone. She also ran teams of girls that could turn a trick, boost, hang paper, fight, stick you up and even fuck you up.

Gypsy was loved by all males, females and those in between - from the major players, the drug dealers, the single mother with eight children to Ned the wino; she was adored by all. She was also an entrepreneur, selling anything …and I mean anything! Drugs, women, guns, you name it. In addition, she could hold hands – I mean she could fight, fist to cuff with the best of them, male or female. She did not take anyone's BS, and, hands down, she was an extremist who had a love for five things: her family (which was always first), drinking grapefruit juice and corn liquor, helping anyone who was down and out and going to The Jug. Three of the four she could do all day long, every day of the week, 24/7. Her fifth love came later on thanks to yours truly Ronald James aka "Daddy Ron".

Oh, before I move on, you may have asked yourself, "What is 'The Jug'?" Let me explain – If you wanted a special cake made like a wedding cake, where would you go? To the baker, right? If you wanted some meat, you would go to the butcher...and if you wanted cold hard cash, you would go to the bank. The Jug was the bank and she loved going to withdraw cash. As far as she was concerned, there was no other game in town that was as sweet. If you want money, just go to The Jug and that was it! If you used a pistol, they would chase and hunt you down; however, if you used a pen, they would tell you to have a nice day and would thank you for doing business with them.

In her opinion, most other ways of getting money was what she called double-hustling. She was about working smarter, not harder. Marvin and I were happy with all that we heard and the progress being made, so we agreed to the terms by giving Gypsy my contact number and the stack of profiles.

I am not sure what happened next because things went so fast. Cheryl started coming over daily because of business. Each time she came, she had my agreed amount of cash and she was always bearing gifts – and I am talking top of the line everything both for me and my place.

Expensive leather gear, dress shoes, silk shirts, curtains and decorative rods, microwave oven, oriental rugs and so on...before I knew it my place became a home. Everything that came through my door was brand new.

Cheryl and I began to build a true friendship, spending hours just talking about life and the business. I was so thankful for all the things she did, and at first, I viewed her as a cougar, but then I started to develop feelings for her that I could not explain. Boom - before I knew it, we had become a hot item!

My curiosity of what she did on a daily basis started to get the best of me and I wanted to be with her just in case something went wrong at The Jug. Up until this point, the only altercation the two of us had was when she was heading out one night and I proposed to go along with her. She turned into a wildcat and then turned on me. She was not pleased with the suggestion and she did not want me to ever be exposed to the game, so I conceded and fell back. It still bothered me she was out there with no one to cover her back.

Although the day did come when an opportunity presented itself and Cheryl was one person short for a run to The Jug. She needed someone to drive. Everything was already set up, but one of her workers got sick. She needed to get there ASAP or lose out on the cash that was there for her, so I volunteered myself. Cheryl had no other choice, so I was in!

Cheryl went over my role with me, explaining that this was not a game. Everyone's life was under my care. I needed to follow all traffic laws at all times. Next, it was my responsibility to route out all the predetermined banks that we would hit. When the workers went into the banks, it was my job to look left, right, and all around for police or anything that looked irregular, weird or out of the norm. My eyes needed to move, not my head, and if anything went wrong, it was the workers job to walk away from us (the car) and make their way into the street walking along with traffic. Then it was on me to drive up behind them and pick them up, otherwise wait curbside until they got in the car. Once I had the worker in the car and all things were safe, it was okay to then proceed to our next location.

This was a big thing for me. Cheryl, on the other hand, was leery and tried more than once to talk me out of it. She said that she could get someone else, but I was not having it. No way! This was a chance of a lifetime and I was not going to miss out on this for anything, so we loaded up and went on our way.

Everything went as scheduled at the first bank and as soon as our worker got into the car, I was driving to our next location. Cheryl was the boss and the banker, and every penny that came into that car was turned over to her. Those were the rules and you did not want to break them.

As we drove off, I noticed how each time Cheryl's eyes remained glued to the front doors until the bank was out of sight. She was always on the look-out for anything that was out of the norm. This was her life and she treated her profession like a scientist - checking everything out and verifying every idea according to those facts. If something was off, she aborted the mission.

My first day driving went over as a complete success. I received my $500 cash for the use of the profile, the $200 for driving and then a worker gave me $100 tip. I earned a quick $800 and was blown away to earn this kind of cash while having fun. I loved it and wanted more.

The excitement alone was a high, plus we stopped and ate out and then we were off to the houses of some of Cheryl's friends. She introduced me to everyone at the house, but I had little to say. I was not clear of my role yet, including the status of our relationship.

However, after Cheryl officially moved to my place with one of her loving daughters, Mimi, there was no more room for second guessing. Cheryl sat me down and explained we needed to switch up a few things. She wanted to stay ahead of the game and not make it hot - meaning whoever was hot on our trail would eventually put one and one together and link me as the provider of those profiles.

She always wanted to keep a hedge of protection around

me, plus she wanted to change checks, as well as ID's. What I saw next almost cured me from ever wanting anything else to do with Cheryl and crime. (Notice I said 'almost'!)

She pulled out two large Samsonite suitcases full of every imaginable form of identification you could think of. There were blank birth certificates, social security cards, voter cards, library ID's, baptismal certificates, assortments of work ID's from janitorial to government. There were international and US driver licenses from every nationality, race and sex. That was just the beginning.

There was a paymaster machine that was used to print checks. There was a rainbow assortment of different colored checks from personal accounts, companies that were out of business (some of which may have been closed for ten or more years), and there were current corporate checks on top of it all. She had her hands on government IRS income tax return checks that were the real deal – blank and ready to go.

Anything that had to do with forgery was in those suitcases. She made it clear that if we got busted with this, we would never see the light of day. She kept everything she got her hands on and from time to time, she would recycle things to stay a step ahead of the game. She said, "In order to keep them guessing, you need to change up your work."

Cheryl showed me how to handle paper checks. I was taught to never touch the surface of anything, only the edges. I had many questions and she took the time to give me all the answers from the who, what, where, why and how of the game.

One of my first questions was why did she not just use all the personal checks and go shopping? The answer was clear – there was no money in that. She said the personal check part of the game was meant to be used after you had taken the cash from the account. Then, and only then, is when you go out on the town and treat yourself to whatever the checks could buy. That included fine dining, clothes, furniture and whatever you wanted to buy to make yourself happy.

By far, personal checks were the easiest to do and the quickest to set up; however, the payoff was small. On the other hand, if you set things up correctly, The Jug was the place to be and the cash money was there for the taking.

I asked Cheryl how in the world she accumulated all those items. Anyone else who might have dared to ask this question would have had a bad day, but there are advantages to sleeping with the boss. She explained first that this was not the entire inventory of her stuff. She had a few stash spots around the city with a whole lot more contained there.

I was truly blown away and I could see now why she was called Gypsy. She moved around a lot. So, the same way I met her through George Diggs in Logan, is the way she met others - networking and word of mouth. Everyone who came to her had something for her.

It did not matter what it was, she would work with that person to buy it or use it. Those who came across checks, ID's or anything else in her field, she purchased those items, or at least took a look at them. The only thing that she required you give to her was the history of the item. She needed to know the original source, the prior owners and was it already in use or how recently it had been used.

She did not want to come behind someone else's work – meaning established work that already set the paper trail ablaze. It did not bother her if it was hot and someone else had used it, nor did it mean she would not purchase it. No problem - she would get it, store it in her personal archives for use at a later date, and this was the reason for the suitcases.

Cheryl explained with Philadelphia being circle town, anything happening would sooner or later come around to all the major players, con artist, and gangsters. She made stops to all of the above by way of what she called Traps. By stopping at shooting galleries, speak easies, the projects, bars, after hour clubs, number houses and individual homes, she knew someone had something for her.

Everyone seemed to love this woman they called Gypsy. No matter where we went, young and old, from the professional business owner to the dope fiend, Gypsy's name truly rang bells. Her charisma took center stage, but what kept everyone happy was her genuine charity and kindness for people.

It did not matter who you were or what problem you were having, she would turn her pockets inside out to assist whoever she could whenever she could. That clearly meant the heroin user who needed his/her next fix to the three little boys sitting on the step looking hungry and needed something to eat. Yes, Gypsy would feed them, and if they needed sneakers and she felt moved, they may very well end up with brand new Air Jordan's.

No one escaped her kindness unless you chose to lie or cheat her, or come with game because you would walk away with an ear full of thunder from her rage…or she might hall off and punch you dead in your mouth. Even after all of that, if you came back with respect and corrected your wrong, you may very well get what you initially came for.

After going through all of her stuff, I just could not understand why she did not get rid of some of the things and throw them in the trash. Boy was I green! She told me that she collected most of those items from the trash! She said I would be surprised to see what people throw away as trash, explaining that she once found $10,000.

One day she was dead broke and just when she thought to go into her bag of tricks, she suddenly looked down in someone's trashcan and saw a bank statement and other papers that looked important, so she loaded all the trash into her car. Low and behold, after checking things out, there was enough information for her to run into The Jug and withdraw the $10,000 that showed on the statement – it was just that simple.

Gypsy utilized her entire network to gain access to more work – checks, credit cards and ID's. A young boy had dipped into someone's house recently. All he had time to take was a single piece of paper - one blank personal check - and a few forms of non-essential identification; things I would have thrown into the trash. Cheryl thought this was a gold mine! We paid our cat burglar friend off with a few dollars too much and he left.

I watched as Cheryl went deep into thought and then into action. She picked up the phone and tried to contact a few of her workers who could run into The Jug. Her plan was to call the bank to verify funds and then she would forge the signature that she got off of those non-essential forms of ID that I believed to be trash.

Next, she would make it payable to someone for cash, but we ran into a problem. For some reason, that day she could not locate anyone to make the run with her. Time was running out and it was of the essence. She knew anything could go wrong and the faster we could make the move the better.

So I suggested that I could cash the check - how hard could it be to cash a check? I cashed them all the time when they were my own. Cheryl looked deep in my eyes and what I saw for the first time in our relationship was the love she truly had for me. She put aside her love for the game and said, "No, absolutely not."

Had it been anyone else, she would not have taken a second thought to get the money, but she had always kept me out of the game for my own good. However, it was time and I felt right about being a part of the team, so I spoke up for myself. She asked me in her motherly voice "Are you sure that you want to do this?" She explained that we had so much to lose, but I assured her that I was up for the challenge. Like a boy gazing into his mother's eyes on his first day of school to reassure her that everything would be ok, I said, "Yes".

Well, Cheryl pulled out her good 'ole suitcases with all the fixings and then she ran through about thirty male drivers' licenses before she found one that matched my description. She then forged the signature of the person I was about to play. She told me to memorize my new name, say it over and over again out loud, and then she gave me the math.

Cashing checks is an art form made easy if your ducks are lined up in a row. If you follow the ABC's of forging, you will have no problems, which of course meant you had to have good paper, a live account and solid ID.

It was to your benefit to always know as much as possible about the person you were about to play. It was even more important to know the psychology behind the banking business. She went on to explain what she dubbed the nine categories of cashing a check at The Jug: Young white girls, young white boys, young black girls, middle aged white males and females, middle aged black females, older white women, foreigners, and last but not least, those 'Negro's' – meaning all black males.

If you were to look at these categories on a scale from one to nine (1-9), with one (1) being the easiest to pass a bad/

forged check through, and nine (9) being the person to avoid at all cost, young white girls are one (1) and the black males are nine (9). For the most part, the system was fool-proof and summed up the ease and possibility of cashing forged checks with little to no problems; it also worked in stores when passing personal checks.

Now the system was explained like this – young white girls were very assertive by nature and took charge. They were willing to call the shots and were not afraid to make a mistake. The young white male was eager to make his mark, but at the same time his thoughts was usually elsewhere (sex, his car, or what he would do after work). If things looked in order, he was ok with it.

Next in line was the young black female and she, too, was eager, but she fell in line with any simple command. Her concerns were not to be belittled or challenged by either the customer or a manager. She had something to prove, but not make trouble for herself. Then you have the middle-aged white males and females who have been taught that the customer is always right. However, their concern now was their careers so they would always follow proper bank procedure.

Now the middle aged black woman was proud of her position and, with an attitude, she guarded it with her life. She wanted everyone to know that she would follow bank procedures to a T. If things were in order with your papers, she would follow protocol; however, one thing out of place, missing or odd, and she would have the manager standing beside her in one hot second.

Now, let me share about the older white woman...yes, you know the one... well into her fifties, very professional, starched and does everything methodical. Often times she is very impersonal as she peers at you over her reading glasses that sit at the edge of her nose. She gives you a look that seems to question your every move. Not only does she make you feel this way, she would even question the actions of the bank president! Listen, you would have trouble with her even trying to cash your own check, let alone trying to make any transactions of any kind concerning the game. Yes, the little old white woman will make sure that every 'I' is dotted and every 'T' is crossed. Cheryl made it clear for me to stay away from this group.

Then there were the foreigners and this group was too unpredictable. What was most dangerous about them was their indecisiveness and that always landed them in the company of you know who – the older white woman, even when the older woman was nowhere to be seen. She would pop up at the first sign of a problem, so it did not pay to go this route either.

Now let us take a look at the black male, which was touched on just a bit earlier. The Negro - it did not matter what age he was – he was the worst. Call him super cop, super teller or superman – his JOB was to prove that you were a con, a crook or a liar. He checked your walk when you came through the door. He heard you talk before you opened your mouth and you could make damn sure he was going to check your ID. Hell, he would push your anger button, push you to the ground, and hold you until the cops come if need be.

To top things off, even if your work was in the finest of order, he still was going to get the older white woman to sign off on everything, so going to him was dead and a total waste of time. Now that was the math of check cashing, but she was not done.

Cheryl gave me a number of exit lines just in case the teller was taking too long or something went wrong, such as, "Miss, could you please hurry up because I'm double parked?" "Miss, could you please speed things up? I left my daughter in the car alone." "Sir, will this take much longer? I need to get back to work." And finally, if things seem to be going awry, I would ask for the check back with "Miss, I will take the check to my own bank."

Cheryl also told me to keep coin change in my front pocket. This was an old George Diggs trick. That way when I got in line and a teller window opened up and I saw the middle aged black female, the older white woman, the foreigner or the superman black male, I could drop the change on the floor, forcing the person behind me to go ahead of me. One thing I was told was that people hated to stand in bank lines so whoever was next would kindly jump ahead.

Well, I was all set. I had everything I needed – ID, change, the check, Cheryl's directions on the math, my exit lines, her blessings and an ice cold beer that I slammed down. Now I was ready!

Cheryl drove north on Germantown Avenue towards Chestnut Hill. The bank was located directly on the avenue, so she had to park farther down the street. I could see she was focused, yet nervous for the both of us, but I was cool. Cheryl let me know how things were going to go, but this time she added I should not worry if the teller walks away and takes the check – they are only checking the signature on the bank's microfilm. She assured me if they go there, I will get the money. Why? Cheryl truly was a master forger and studied signatures as a craft! There was no way anything could go wrong. I received my last instruction from Cheryl, which was to follow the same direction we gave to others who went into The Jug…if there was a problem, do not walk to the car.

With a $500 check in my hand, I headed into the bank. Instantaneously I transformed into my new character. In the memo of the check it was noted that I had done some construction work for Mrs. Such and Such and I was at the bank to collect my $500 fee.

I quickly jumped in line and scanned the tellers at the windows to determine which one would be best suited for me to go to. There was no need for the pocket change distraction this day. I observed two young white girls, a young white male, and a middle aged white woman. No problems here.

When it was my turn, I stepped in front of one of the two young white girls located right in the center of all the action. I smiled and she smiled back and then I spoke, keeping my conversation to just a hello (I recalled what George Diggs told me about over playing). She was very pleasant and asked how she could help me. I quickly took out my pen and acted like I signed the back of the check in front of her. Deception was key and worked like magic, and then I slid the check to her, along with my now assumed driver license and other form of ID.

She went through the mechanics of processing the check, flipping the check over looking at my signature and my ID. I thought this was going to be a walk in the park...that was until she walked away. Then I remembered the signature file check at the microfilm.

What was a few minutes seemed to be a lifetime. I thought about getting the hell out of that bank, but Cheryl's golden rule was never to leave any of the work behind so I stayed put. Just that quickly, things went from bad to worse because out of nowhere appeared the older white woman...this party was over folks! I knew something was about to go down and I had started to sweat.

The white young girl returned with a smile and asked me how would I like my money. Whew! Interception avoided and the older white woman disappeared as quickly as she had appeared. However, anxiety had formed moisture at the top of my head. I could feel it acuminating in one part of my scalp. Beads of sweat began to work their way past each strand of my hair, building up momentum as it made its way to my forehead. My answer to her question was "large bills please".

I was in the midst of a rush – I was high and enjoying this feeling of living on the edge and it was crazy. Part of me was saying, "RUN!" and the other part calmly said, "Stay, this is what it's all about." This internal struggle became a place I craved and every time I experienced it, I wanted more of it.

As the teller counted and recounted the money, the feeling of victory started to take over and when she passed me the money, simultaneously a bead of sweat rolled off my forehead down my nose and onto the cash. I thanked the teller and made a one hundred and eighty degree turn for the exit.

Meanwhile, Cheryl was doing some sweating of her own. She was fussing with herself on how foolish she was to consent for me to go into The Jug, but it was too late since I was already out and into the car with cash in hand. She gave me a big 'ole kiss and then stuck out her hand. She went right back to business and said, "Hand me the money".

I did not mind one bit. I received a double pay-off. I got the cash and I got high while doing it. When I went into the bank, I felt one way; however, the feelings I got when I came out were hard to explain other than to tell you I was high. I was on a roll…or so I thought.

I started going into the banks more often, and I began to write personal checks like they were going out of style.

Cheryl told me to cool out, saying it was okay to do personal checks, but not at the rate I was doing them. First of all, that part of the game was set aside strictly for pleasure. In addition, everyone and their mother were now making the game hot by doing them. I was told that there were now instant electronic checking systems and, if I played them correctly, I could run the gambit and make a killing.

Cheryl broke it down like this – the mother of all checking systems was Telecheck. Then there were JBS, JBC, Welcome Check, Check USA, In-House Checking System and a host of others. She explained the ins and outs of all these and what we needed to do to stay ahead of them.

Lastly, she said there was no money in that game and the sooner I realized it, the better off I would be. Hands down the money was in The Jug. It would take time to set things up and do them right to avoid getting hung up on the electronic TeleCheck system. I wanted the feeling of the rush of being high, on the edge, so I found patience. She continued explaining what we needed to do before we went too much farther with the game.

Then, out of nowhere, as if Cheryl was on her own reality show, she began to dance and sing her theme song by Ashford and Simpson, "Take it to the Bank". We laughed as I received her message and changed my tune.

Under her direction, I went into The Jug a few more times, but when the music stopped playing, she did not want me doing that anymore. Therefore, I put it to rest and reassumed my role as driver for the next several months.

By Christmas time 1985 through March 31, 1986, I was back in full swing as the person hitting The Jug several times a day. I was loving it and living large! We were doing it big time and the basement of my place could not hold anything else.

Having money and all these things gave me a sense of power. However and unlike Cheryl, who gave to anyone from the heart, I enjoyed giving for the feeling of power, pride, and to get something in return. One of the things I found out about giving was that it made me feel good, but only for a short period. I was just as guilty as the beggar, the thief or anyone who thought they were getting over on me – that was because I was looking for something in return.

Whether or not my ego was stroked by feeling important, or I had a motive for you to do something for me later, not all the giving I did was out of a pure heart. I used you, you used me; we were just one big selfish family. The only thing different was that I was not running around in a large purple dinosaur suit; I wore a mask instead, one that hid my true self…one that I thought would allow me to hid from who I really was.

We were returning from Virginia when Cheryl and I stopped in Delaware to hit The Jug and it paid off. We each ended up with $3,400 in our pockets! However, even with lots of nice things and money in hand, I had lost sight of my goals. Why was my mind focused on just one more hit? I should have paid attention to Cheryl and left the game alone. My life was about to crash and crash real hard.

It was a sunny day in Philadelphia, a clear day on May 14, 1986. It was probably five or six o'clock in the afternoon when we drove up to our place on Germantown Avenue. I distinctly remember this day because I could not wait to get inside to get my grub on – I was so hungry and there was a steak calling my name

After parking the car in front of the house, we were immediately approached by the numbers writer, who casually walked up to us from across the street. He said, "Ron, Gypsy,

111

I'm not sure what's going on, but for the last two days my people have been telling me that these two crackers have been camped out in that green unmarked car up the street behind you. They must be Five-O (police) because I saw them pop up with their binoculars. Yea, they are cops alright, I'm sure of it." I thanked him for his loyalty and the heads up.

Yo, Hello Ron, is anyone home? Now I just heard what the numbers writer said. The warning was as clear as it was outside that day, yet my focus was on self and getting something in my stomach.

Cheryl was moving fast. She went in the house before me, it was as if she heard the message loud and clear. I went to the kitchen while Cheryl ran upstairs. I placed two T-bone steaks in the broiler and opened a bottle of beer. I took a sip and it was about this time Cheryl poked her head into the kitchen to tell me that she would be right back. She said she needed to make a run. I tried to slow her down by telling her that I had two steaks on, but she said she was fine and then said "I'm out."

Before she got out the door, she then hit me with a profound statement, "Let me hold the money." I looked at her as if she was crazy and shared a similar statement back to her, "NO! Let me hold yours instead." We laughed and I checked on my meal.

As she headed for the front door, I followed her out, walked her to the car and gave her a kiss as I opened the driver's side door for her. I walked back to the sidewalk, looking up the street and recalling what the numbers man warned me of. I stood there searching for these so-called white undercover police in the green unmarked car and, just like he said, there they were and we had the pleasure of simultaneously spotting each other. It was on!

Their car jumped out into traffic, while I turned and started to walk down the street. At the same time, Cheryl had been watching me and tried to turn around to block them off. She did not get there in time and had to continue driving past me. They pulled right up next to me and the two officers quickly jumped out and identified themselves as police. One of them said, "Is your name Ronald James?" I sounded off with, "Why are you looking for my brother?" The next question was "Do you have any ID?" I told them no.

The truth was I had given all the work back to Cheryl when I came out of The Jug in Delaware. The only thing in my possession was cash. The other cop told me to place my hands on the car. My reply was very assuring, "No problem officer." As soon as my hands touched their vehicle, my feet sprung into action! I took flight like a jet, catch me if you can. I was out of there…if these two jokers thought they were going to lock up Ronald James today, they had another thing coming!

I was off and running, darting right past Cheryl and our souped-up Dodge Dart. I figured Cheryl would pull off and circle the block to scoop me up somewhere around the corner. I ran straight down the middle of Germantown Avenue between traffic. I could hear the flat foots coming up behind me. They were closing in when they made the call for back up. "We're in pursuit of a black male, on foot, six foot three inches tall, heading south on Germantown Avenue". Then I changed the game and ran directly in front of a car in on-coming traffic and then shot down Philellena next to the deli.

I continued on with my lead sizable enough now that I should have stopped into the deli to order a Philly cheese steak and some fries to go. This was going to be a long day for the 'ole donut boys. I knew I could easily lose them once I hit the alley; however, after making a quick left and another left into an alley, I realized that I just ran into a dead end! When I turned around to run back onto the street, the first cop had already shot past me, while the other one ran directly into me as I was exiting the alley.

Within seconds, these Keystone Cops had me cuffed and headed to the crowd that had now formed. I did not realize I had so many people in that neighborhood on my side. There had to be at least 10 bystanders wanting to make sure I received fair justice and not Philadelphia justice. Trust me, once you give the boys a run for their money they make sure you pay, very unpleasantly, especially if you out stomp them out.

Well, I was marched to the top of Germantown Avenue and there awaiting me was a patrol car with its lights flashing. Immediately my pockets were turned inside out and to the surprise of the Philly detective, he found a wad of crisp one hundred dollar bills in my left pocket. He began counting them off aloud: one, two…seventeen, eighteen… thirty three, thirty four hundred dollars to be exact, and in my right pocket I had a few hundred dollars more.

He was upset about being made to chase me, so he barked into the crowd of on lookers, "Oh what do we have here…a drug dealer!" I was placed into the cop car and taken to the 35th District. Apparently, the Philadelphia police were working in conjunction with the Abington Police Department out of Montgomery County, PA. They received a profile on me and were investigating my activities concerning bad checks. Imagine that!

Well, there I sat in that cold, dark holding tank with someone who smelled like crap. I was very unclear and uncertain as to what was going on. My mind was racing and all I knew was I needed to get the hell out of that place and get on with my life. What I did not realize was that I was in for a number of rude awakenings that day, starting with the Philadelphia Police Department.

They had nothing on me, but they were going to put me through the processing before they turned me over to Abington. Abington was not about to let me get out on bail because they knew that I had cash, so they told me when I did see the judge that my bail would be set sky high. Next, they told me that I would not be going anywhere anytime soon because I had a violation of probation in Montgomery County. I was confused and asked them about this violation of probation and they kindly offered an explanation. I had a theft by unlawful taking in Lansdale, Montgomery County, PA that had not yet expired. Yes, 17 days shy of completion. Go figure!

After what seemed like hours in the Philadelphia Police Department, I was taken out of the holding pen, photographed, finger printed and asked about 100 questions. They wanted to know my full name, address, date of birth, parent's info, did I have any scars or marks due to any injuries or any identifiable marks like tattoos, was I on drugs, prescriptions or otherwise.

As I sat handcuffed to a bench, the questions kept coming, and not just by them. I kept asking myself a lot of questions about my current situation and what led me to this. They had taken my shoes and my belt, I guess so I could not kill myself, and what I recall most was that I was cold and hungry.

Things somehow rolled into the following day and finally I went before a video screen and faced a judge who had more questions and told me that I would be going with the Abington Police, after which they would be transporting me to Montgomery County. I was still unclear and wanted to know what was going on with my bail so that I could be released. It was confirmed that there was absolutely no reason for me to be concerned about any of that. Montgomery County had already lodged a detainer for my probation violation that stopped my release. I would have to answer to a judge there to resolve that issue.

By this time I was exhausted behind all of the unwanted excitement. I was still confused as to why I could not be released; not all the money in the world could set me free. I felt dirty and wanted to get in my own shower and rinse off. My wrist was aching from the pressure being applied from the metal designer bracelets police and law enforcement called handcuffs. They dug into my skin and left an impression on my wrist that lasted for hours...both in my flesh and in my mind. I was at my wits end.

I need to interject something here – up to this point in time, I had really never experienced being locked up with the shackle and handcuff combination. Either one of them in their own right serves its purpose of gaining control of a person by means of confinement, but the combination of the two was just grizzly.

Fetters, shackles or whatever you choose to call them have been around since the ancient times of slavery and, in my opinion, there is something that takes place both psychologically and physiologically to any person who has ever had to endure this form of punishment. It is unjust, inhumane and unnatural to the free spirit. The very sound of each click of metal that closes on you feels like a mortification of your being. Freedom disappears and bondage is made clear. However, the combination of shackles and handcuffs made me feel barbaric; animal like. This was nothing more than modern day slavery. By no means am I trying to pull a race card and justify any of my criminal behavior...No Way!

I believe that there is a bigger picture and I will address my concerns later, but for now, back to the processing.

I was loaded into the back of police vehicle, hog tied, if you will and transported to Abington Township Police Department. I ended up lying sideways on the seat, in a half twisted position. When I awoke from my sleep, I did not recall the ride, but I definitely felt the muscle cramps and stiffness that had set in. I did, however, also recall being very hungry and thought to myself how good those two steaks would have been, but I never got to take them out of the broiler. See, just me thinking about me again!

What I got from the Abington Police Department was some of the same treatment I received from the Philadelphia Police Station, only worse. The same being photographed, finger printed, and lots of lots of questions. The worst being that they pressed me for details and a confession. When I asked them could I make a phone call – you know, just like you see happen on television – I was told I would be given that call as soon as what needed to be done was done. When I asked about my money, I was told I would get a receipt. When I asked if I could get something to eat, I was told the next shift handled meals.

The police seemed to have all the answers without doing anything that I wanted or needed done. The police had their own style of psycho-babble and spin that kept you guessing. When you caught wind of it and tried to confront them by calling them on their stuff, they simply switched their game and became forceful and physical. When you pressed the issue further, you could very well end up with some additional trumped-up charges in addition to the ass whipping they just gave you.

I spent most of my time in a holding pen where I sat and

sat for hours with nothing to do and no one to talk to because you were not allowed to talk. The room was ice cold and there were no pillows or blankets… nothing except a partially used roll of toilet tissue that allowed me to somewhat prop my head up as I laid there on a sheet of cold hard steel.

My hunger pains started to get the best of me and I began to softly cry out, "Officer, officer" over and over again. I repeated myself hoping to gain a response. After no one responded to my call, I raised my voice louder and louder to the point that I was yelling, and then I began to bang on the metal bunk. After trying for well over an hour, I finally got someone's attention. A cop came back and asked me "What the hell was my problem?" I explained that I had not eaten since I got locked up and begged him for something to eat. He told me it was not his fault that I missed out, and that it was the responsibility of the last shift to handle the feeding.

I was spun at this point, but my only problem was I had no idea who was doing the spinning. Was it this guy or someone from the previous shift? My attitude and feelings were such that I wanted to alert the President of the United States and let him know just how these law enforcement officers where mistreating me. However, my feelings did not matter because I was not going to get anything to eat until I reached the prison…or so I was told.

The Prison?! What in the world was this officer talking about? Prison was for criminals and what would a prison have to do with me? For whatever reason, I was no longer hungry because of the unknown fear that so abruptly gripped me, taking hold of both my gut and my mind. How could all of this be happening to me? All I wanted was my beer and that delicious steak off the broiler. There in the quietness of my heart I cried out, asking God to please help me. I said my foxhole prayer and waited for results.

"James", the officer barked and I jumped to my feet and said, "Yes sir." I was told to come out and put on my shoes. I was still in shock, but I moved quickly as he escorted me to another officer who re-fitted me with handcuffs and shackles. Then I was placed in the back of a police cruiser that was very uncomfortable for my six foot three inch frame, plus this time my arms were handcuffed behind my back and it was extremely painful.

I dealt with the pain the best way I could – by sitting sideways. I felt crammed, caged in, nauseous, anxious and, to top it off, I could smell the perspiration of myself from the past countless hours of anxiety and fear…and my hunger pains had returned with a vengeance! I thought to myself….what on earth could be next?!

During intake at the prison I was hit with another onslaught of questions, some of the same ones the police had already asked me. Again, I was photographed and fingerprinted. I was told to strip, butt-hole naked…yes, you heard me…right down to my birthday suit so that another grown man could inspect me. I was humiliated beyond words. I had to stand there in front of him while he ordered me to move my body parts around, peering at my genitals. He even told me to turn away from him, bend over and stick my butt in his face so that he could inspect the crack of my asshole. Trust me, after not showering for the past twenty-four hours, that was not the place any one needed to sticking their face!!

After all of that, I felt dehumanized and defeated. I did feel better after getting a shower and something to eat. All my personal belongings were packed up, I was issued a set of prison clothing, a set of sheets and a blanket, but not much else. The prison was located at 35 East Airy Street, Norristown PA. I am not sure when the place was built, but the face of the building was literally like a stone castle that matched the cell they put me in. To me, that place felt like a dungeon. I was in the Intake part of the jail in a large cell with three other men and bunk beds. No phone calls, little movement, not much to eat and not allowed to talk to the others or ask questions of the guards.

The jail itself had a very cold, eerie feeling about it. It was old and archaic, yet it functioned rather smooth with only a population of about six hundred men. Prison had its own pecking order that was established by the inmates. If you were in prison on charges of larceny or theft, you faired close to the top. The same was true if you were a drug dealer. However, all of that was subject to change if you were a drug king pin, or if you were locked up for a large amount of money, or a chunk of charges. Most of those inmates could set the rules of what went on in the prison.

In the far right cellblocks, you had those who were in jail for armed robbery and others who were charged with murder. I say "charged" only because none of them totally put all their business out to others as if they were guilty, yet they wanted everyone to believe they were killers to keep the real killers off them.

Then there were those who were very unfortunate to fall on the far left. This was anyone with a case of rape or even worse – those who were charged with child molesting or crimes against children. No amount of money could save them from the brunt of what prison life had to offer. They were beat up, spit on and tormented, plus, anything of value that they owned was usually taken. Most, if not all, chose to take protective custody and remain away from the general population of the prison.

From what I could tell, the jail ran itself – meaning the prisoners ran the jail. I could not wait to catch up with a guy I just met by the name of Willie and when I did, I found him sitting next to the twenty foot prison wall that surrounded the yard. He was glad to see me, but not as relieved as I was to find him. I could tell by his demeanor that this was certainly not his first rodeo.

When I sat down with him, he was very open, helpful and willing to give me the math on prison life. The rules were simple to understand: 1) Don't trust anyone 2) Don't borrow anything 3) Don't gamble 4) Don't mess with the [faggots]. Not long after that, I found out there was a fifth rule that had not been mentioned. Maybe because it was an understood rule to those who knew the system, but the rule everyone in prison mainly focused on was respect...and its direct opposite - disrespect.

If you disrespected someone, you became fair game and you could be killed because of it. Disrespect said, 'I don't give a damn about you', which in prison literally meant 'bring on the noise, the drama and anything else you got... oh, and fuck you, too!'

Once you disrespected someone, that person was most often forced to do something. His choices were simple – he could accept it, which almost NEVER happened, or he could do the same back to you and close the door of disrespect to show others in the jail to not walk through it. Another thing I noticed was that it did not take long for news to travel throughout the jail. Jail news was like an in-house grapevine and, in my opinion, this form of communication reached the masses almost as fast as the internet. Point being…if you disrespected someone, the word got out and got out fast!

Willie and I sat back and got to know each other. I found out that he was from North Philly and he had done time before up state at both Dallas and Graterford. He had also done time in the Philadelphia System at Homesburg and in New York on Rikers Island, both of which were cut throat, killer jails…I mean no joke, Willie was truly a seasoned convict.

I never really knew why he was in prison, but it was clear that he was a stick-up boy, or a Brody boy, who is someone who takes what he wants from whoever he wants when he wants, and he was not to be toyed with.

The prison was made up of mainly blacks and whites, and I would have to say it was a pretty even ratio. There were also Spanish, but no one group ran the jail; it was more the presence of who had the drugs or connections. Everything was done at a price and no one did anything for free. If you wanted a haircut, extra food, your clothes washed, folded or pressed you paid a price. Most of the time, your pay would be in the form of smokes or food from the commissary.

Jail seemed to be the classic 'keeping up with the Jones" scene and everything was pay as you go, with the exception of the jail house stores. It had a number of stores and it consisted of someone selling commissary items at an inflated interest rate. Anyone could run a store, but you had better know what you were doing to keep it. Why?…

In jail there was always someone who was willing to try you, or you could be set up for guards to run in on you, or there was the person who would fight you for yours…not to mention all the lies that con men would promise on Friday when their release date was on Thursday! The rates were mainly two-for-one, meaning you get one item today and, on store day, you pay back two of the same items. Some of the stores would do two-for-three or even three-for-five, but the money was in the two-for-one.

Prison life also had its own jargon. For the first time in my life I heard the words "chumpy" or "jon". Both words meant nothing, yet they meant the exact same thing. For example, I asked my cellie to pass me the jon (soap, cup, sheet of paper, pencil, candy bar...or anything) and he knew what I was talking about and passed it to me. The same was true with the word chumpy. Meaning, I am going out to the chumpy (yard, dayroom, visit) and again the crazy thing about it was that everyone knew just what the other person meant.

I was getting antsy and wanted to know what was going on with my case. I had been out to court and Abington stuck it to me. They cleaned up their books with any and all the forgeries I posted in their township and in Cheltenham Township, which was next door to them. When it was all said and done, I received charges from:

Abington Police Department: charged with 5 cases of forgery, 4 cases of theft by deception, one case of retail theft and 2 cases of receiving stolen property;

Montgomery Township Police Department: charged with 2 cases of forgery, one case of theft by deception and one case of receiving stolen property;

Ambler Police Department: charged with 2 cases of forgery, one case of theft by deception and one case of retail theft;

Upper Gwynedd Township Police Department: jumped on board with 2 more cases of forgery and one case of theft by deception;

Lansdale and Hatfield Township: did a combination at the

Magistrates Office with 3 cases of forgeries, 2 cases of bad checks, 2 cases of theft by deception, 2 cases of receiving stolen property, and then a conspiracy charge surfaced in Bucks County that I was certain was not mine.

<u>Warminster Township Police Department</u>: charged with one case each of forgery, theft by unlawful taking or disposition, bad check and receiving stolen property. They claimed I went into a local branch of a bank in Doylestown, PA and dropped a check for a few thousand dollars and walked out with the money. Well, I know for a fact that was a lie. They even said they had my photo, which was another lie. I know, without a doubt, they had nothing on me. If they had anyone on video it was one of our workers whom Cheryl had sent into The Jug. Yes, I was on the scene, but I was the driver and did not go into The Jug, and with that admission, Philadelphia had found something on me after all and they charged me with forgery, retail theft, receiving stolen property, theft by deception, bad checks and arrest prior to requisition - whatever that meant. Fortunately, I had the money to pay for an attorney.

One day when I was talking with Cheryl, she told me that when she did time in federal prison something amazing happed to her. Someone had suggested that if she were to read from the Bible in the Book of Psalms, Chapter's 1, 23 and 70 once a day, she would gain God's favor, find peace, and be set free. Well, with me going to court every other day and feeling low, stressed and perplexed, I welcomed her suggestion. All I needed to do was do what Cheryl did and I would be set free.

So with a new plan of action, I set out to get a Bible. I would have been satisfied with one of those plain Gideon

Bibles, but what I received was a King James Version, and if it was good for the King, it was good for me!

Up to this point, I still held on to those resentments I had from the fourth grade when my classmates laughed at me, so when I read, I made certain I was by myself and no one could make fun of me. Moreover, this reading was different. Reading these verses meant I was going to get some type of reward or blessing for reading. I was going to be set free...yes! I had faith. I started out with Psalms 23 and I enjoyed those words because they were so soothing. I read Psalms 1, 23 and 70 each day for about a week.

When I told Cheryl, she instructed me to keep up the good work. Then one day I got the notion to read it twice a day because I was looking for a double blessing. I had so much faith with what I was doing I turned it up to three times a day and, before I knew it, I was able to read the verses from memory. Then I began to add Psalms 103 and I could tell blessings were on their way.

On November 17, 1986, I, Ronald Lloyd James, went before Judge Yohn in front of a packed courtroom of family and friends and three people took the stand on my behalf – my brother John, my former elementary school principal and a catholic priest who had befriended me because I went to a few of his services in jail. My childhood friend's father told me well in advance that I had the judge's favor. You see, he had spoken with the judge off the record and revealed to me that the judge was good natured.

That day in the courtroom, I watched as the judge excused himself to his chambers and I noticed that, even though my life was on the line with charges that could potentially amount to 20 plus years upstate, this was a game to the attorneys.

What I meant by that statement was this: my lawyer,

who was well paid, said he knew the judge and the district attorney, and when it came down to it, he really did not do a lot for me. He basically accepted my money, told me to follow his lead in hopes of a lighter sentence by throwing myself on the mercy of the court, and to try to show compassion when the judge spoke to me.

The next thing I noticed was this: the District Attorney, who was called a friend of my attorney, came over to me right before the court proceedings and tried to wheel and deal without my attorney present. He made me an offer of five to ten years if I said 'yes' right then. This was supposed to be a much better deal than the seven to fourteen year deal he previously offered. I very well might have taken his offer of five years if #1) I did not have a lawyer who had my money, and #2) was privy to inside information that the judge was going to go easy on me. The reason being is that some friends had spoken with the judge before sentencing on my behalf. So I thought to myself, "Go kick rocks, Mr. District Attorney – today is not your day for making deals".

Then there was the master of ceremonies, "The Judge". Was he in on this game, too? You can bet your bottom dollar he was. It was not me that he cared so much about, no way! It was the word of someone he respected and/or was his supporter during re-election time. What made his decision easy were all the letters of support on my behalf, those who took the stand and a packed courtroom of childhood classmates and friends, business owners, professionals and family. Yes, this is what helped him to justify what he had already decided he was going to do.

Now, what about me? My intentions were honorable, but my understanding about life was thrown off. In my mind, the only thing that meant anything was to get out of jail.

In plain English…I wanted what I wanted and I wanted it now! I did not care about the victims, including their family members and friends, who got hurt along the way. I never took time to even consider the victims feelings, how I affected them emotionally, or how my actions caused lasting pain that scarred their minds.

I did not care about their financial loss and how I stole not only their physical items, but their loss of control and the way they now may have to treat their customers differently. I will not even mention those I put out of business. My selfish attitude was about to take on a new meaning. The five-year deal that the District Attorney offered me might have done me some good because I had a lot of growing up to do.

Looking back, the only game that was really being played was the one I was playing on myself. Everyone who came to court that day, who wrote letters or spoke on my behalf, genuinely and truly cared about me and believed in me, and I regret that I let all of them down. I apologize now to every one of them for my selfishness. What I failed to realize then was the ability to care about anyone other than myself.

When Judge Yohn emerged from his chambers, he read all of my charges, which seemed to take every bit of an hour. When he was done, he gave me a stern talk and 11-1/2 to 23 month county sentence, plus good time, and that meant I would have to do a total of about 9 months! I felt great because I already had six months in…what a blessing…or was it a curse?

When I got back to the prison, I shared my good fortune with everyone and what I heard from the men was their approval and congratulations. It was the mindset of the inmates that I had achieved something almost like a college degree. The goal of everyone who is in is to get out. My uncle used to say to me, "The only bird that can't fly is a jail bird." Well, it was past time for me to fly, but I continued with the jail routine for a few more months.

It was almost time for me to get out when, through some trusted friends, I got the news that all my money and worldly possessions were gone! I did not understand why and tried to find out from Cheryl what was going on. I found out later that part of what I heard was true. In my eyes, Gypsy had failed me, but the real truth is that is the price everyone pays when they land in jail - you lose something.

My loss was all the money that I had in the banks in Virginia…gone. I am talking $20K, plus my cash stash of $10K that Gypsy was holding onto for me…gone! I was sick about it. I was hurt and my anger was an understatement of what I really felt. My friend who informed me of what had happened continued to tell me that all of my jewelry I had put away in a cigar box…gone! They said that someone other than Gypsy cleaned me out. I demanded to know who and the answer was any one of a number of fleas she was traveling with in her caravan. Oh! I was in my rage bag, but somehow I found forgiveness.

All I can say is love is a strange beast. Plus, Cheryl said and did all of the right things to make me feel pampered. We spent time together and talked, and she said something that reverberated within my soul, "Daddy Ron, we can always get back what was lost and do things better next time."

I looked into her eyes and I was sold on making it work, only this time I specifically told her that I was not going to write any more checks. Then she reminded me with a big smile and her most affectionate voice, "I never wanted you to do anything except be there for me." Well, I could not argue that.

I signed out and was on my way to a new life. I walked out of prison feeling like a new man and when I looked back at the walls that confined me, I thought about all the changes that had taken place. I had been locked up for months and transported from township to prison, back to township, then to the new Montgomery County Prison to their farm program and then to another county jail in Bucks County to complete my course. The sad thing was the one thing that really needed to change remained the same and that was me.

I was standing in front of Bucks County Correctional Facility and I was not going to wait around for family or friends to pick me up. No way! I got the hell out of there on the first thing smoking, which was a Septa Bus, and made my way back to Philly.

On the bus ride home, I had a chance to think and consider life with a new outlook. As I pondered my thoughts, I knew I had to do things in a totally different way, and that was when I had an idea. I thought I would put together a cleaning company. I knew how much I enjoyed working with my high school friend's dad cleaning offices and he had taught me a lot about the business. In addition, I picked up a number of tricks on how to strip, buff and wax floors while in prison. So, just like that, I set my mind on doing something positive and moved in that direction.

As soon as I could, I ran my idea past Cheryl. She was all for it. Therefore, with a new lease on life, and instead of running around writing checks for those things that glittered, I had other people write checks for me. I sent workers into stores to purchase cleaning supplies so we could use the items for our company.

One day my frat brother, Cheryl and I sat down for a business meeting. We talked about going into the janitorial business together. Boy was I excited! The first thing we needed was a name. I came up with the name Jets Janitorial. It had a ring to it and everyone liked it and agreed. I spoke with one of our case lawyers in Center City who drafted up our articles of incorporation. When it was all said and done, we had a bona fide legal corporation, Jets Janitorial and Extermination Company.

Still I was looking for something else. My impulsive nature kicked in and I came up with another bright idea…we should move! I was tired of living in Philly so I spoke with Cheryl about moving out of state and she agreed.

I met up with one of our friends who did wreck chasing to set up our scam so we would have money for the move. (*Sidebar: wreck chasing is a very organized scam that chases the scenes of car accidents. The orchestrator would take charge by placing people who were not involved with the accident at the scene of the accident for the benefit of taking all parties to a lawyer, doctor, hospital or even a dentist for profit.*) This was a sure shot for me to get my hands on a quick $20K. I had been in a number of scams like this and they all paid off. All I needed to do was have an accident with my own car and then allow the insurance company to cover the costs. Please folks, do not try any of what you read here at home – they are all the wrong choices!

I got my wreck chasing friend to crash into my car with one of his cars. He did a nice job on my back side panel, too! I collected the broken plastic from my taillight so that I could scatter it later at the scene of a planned accident. Then one rainy night, that is exactly what I did. I called the police and informed them that a car ran into the back of me while I was parked waiting for the rain to slow down before getting out of the car.

I was theatrical and told the cop that I needed medical attention. This followed Law Suit Course-101 to a tee. The police filed a report, I went to the hospital for treatment, followed by a number of therapy sessions, and finally made our way to an attorney who, by the way, paid us top dollar in front money for taking our case. The attorney promised to settle within six months and he did just that. Cheryl and I were on a natural high and we both felt it was time to move to the next level in our relationship, so on one of our many runs to The Jug down south, we got married! YES! We got married in the small town of Eastville, Virginia with my dad John James as the witness...but the story does not end here. You would think that marriage would have settled me down and I would do all the right things for the woman I loved and to have our happily ever after. Oh no, not Ron James!

CHOICE FIVE
MAGGIE MAE

MY MANIPULATIVE MINDSET AND selfish sexual desires kicked in. I had met a young lady who I could not wait to make a rendezvous with. She was sweet. How sweet, you ask? Think about a Lindors Chocolate Truffle and you will understand just how sweet she was.

For the most part, I was true to my relationship with Cheryl. However, I had a select few days and a select few women with whom I danced with on separate dance floors, and this just happened to be one of those days I wanted to dance with "Lindor". So I told Cheryl that I had an exterminating job that needed my attention because I knew how much she hated the smell of the chemicals. I knew she would not think twice about coming along.

Later that evening, I packed up my exterminating equipment and headed off. On my way to Lindor's place, I picked up some beer because I knew how much she enjoyed drinking…and I knew what a few ice cold beers did for me!

As soon as I got in the door of her apartment, we embraced. Her silky smooth lips and her warm touch literally made me crumble. Her body was firm yet tender. Everything about her in this department was extremely affectionate. She escorted me inside and I handed her the beer and began to get right to work. I exterminated her apartment in no time flat and after I was done, we sat down in the living room area to talk. She then got up and went to the kitchen for glasses for the beer and I sat back and watched her coke-bottle shaped body ease out of sight. Man, this was sweet!

We talked and laughed together as we drank, and then she disappeared again, only this time into the darkness of her hallway. When she came back, she was wearing a see-through silk night gown and the uncontrollable male reaction began. My body responded with massive blood flow, while elevating to the occasion. My heart started racing as I broke out in a light sweat, and just as I began to take control of this situation, I was gently persuaded to sit back and enjoy the ride.

After our moments of tenderness and excitement, we walked back to her bedroom. I thought it was to finish what we had started, but when we reached her bedroom she asked me for a small favor. I was certain it had to do with money and I was correct. She wanted to borrow a few dollars and I did not see any problem with giving Lindor some cash. I felt there was a special bond between us, so I reached into my pocket, pulled out my knot and peeled off a crisp one hundred dollar bill for her. She smiled and thanked me over and over again. She wanted me to know that this was only a loan, but I cut her off and said it was a gift.

Then she revealed to me what I already knew – that she was going to use the money in order to get high. However, I really was not expecting what happened next. She asked me if I could do one more favor for her by driving her across town into the bad lands of 9th Street to cop.

Immediately I was faced with all kinds of choices and my mind raced about what I should do. I had so many bad dealings with drugs and my drug dealing dreams never amounted to anything. My Uncle Pete had an overdose on drugs, my cousin Tyrone was killed in the drug game, my brother John and my cousin Marvin did time for drug sales, Gypsy had run through all my cash because of drugs, and now Lindor wanted me to go cop for her.

I was faced with taking someone I cared about on a drug run. The reality of that situation was simple… kiss the girl and the $100 goodnight, or go cop. Since I was already in bed with her, literally, my allegiance was crystal clear – make the run. Lindor was special, I had her back and I knew she had mine.

So I told her let's go get this done and she got dressed and we raced out the door and into the wind. My heart was beating fast again, only this ride was more like an adventure as it turned into an instant "high". The excitement of doing something wrong and living on the edge proved to be a thrill, which was the same feeling I got when going into The Jug.

Truly at this time in my life, I was totally blinded by self-centeredness. The only person I really cared about was me, not my family, Cheryl, her children and certainly not any of my friends. I was on a slow course towards destruction. I had no fear of God and I loved what I was doing. I was prideful, arrogant, practiced all kinds of evil behaviors and spoke perverse things (Proverbs 8:13). Plus, I was about to eat the fruit of my own way and be filled with their own devices (Proverbs 1:30-31).

The battle over my life was waged in the spiritual realm. I believed I was called to do great things, this book being just one of them, and the evidence of this battle is now manifested in the following pages. As I attempt to share what was very real and what was the realm of life for Ronald James and how I understood it, I need to caution you. The things that are about to be explained may range from bazaar to downright insane.

PLEASE DO NOT TRY THEM! How I survived was only through the grace and mercy of a loving God…and who is to say you will be as fortunate.

Lindor and I returned from our run, we headed back to the safety of her apartment bedroom. I sat at the foot of her bed wondering if I had done the right thing. I am sure the blank stare on my face made her question what was on my mind. I reached into my pocket and presented her with my token of love…the bag of cocaine.

I handed Lindor something that was equivalent to my own death sentence. I gave her the small plastic bag that was sealed air tight. The coke that I was used to was white; however, the color of this coke was yellow, like butter. Lindor's eyes said it all and her face lit up with excitement. She wore a smile that every carved jack-o-lantern on Halloween night would have envied.

I closely watched her as if I was in Chemistry101. Her movements were very systematic, yet graceful. She worked off a TV dinner tray. Reaching under her bed, she pulled out a small shoebox and removed the lid. It appeared to me, and probably to the average person, that its contents were nothing but junk, and I was sadly mistaken.

The first thing to emerge was none other than a small bricker brack glass pipe, just like the one I first saw in California. Next was a glass vial that had a bread tie wrapped around the top, which served as a handle. There were also a number of small matchbooks, a rag and broken pieces of wire from a coat hanger.

I was used to seeing people smoke crack, but I never really watched the full procedure up close. I had a bird's eye view and was as inquisitive as a student watching the professor in a laboratory; fully consumed. I wanted to know what was next.

Lindor jumped up from her seated position on her bed and, without warning, left the room with the coke in her hand, only to quickly return with a small cup of water she had gotten from the bathroom. She then tore the back off from a matchbook and creased it down the middle, sitting it on the table. With another piece of cardboard, she dipped it into the baggie and removed a small portion of the yellowish substance and placed it on the folded matchbook cover.

Tilting the matchbook cover at the opening of the glass vial, she carefully tapped in all the coke. She then raised the vial in the air to her eye level and shook it to even out the coke inside. While holding the vial with her left hand, she dipped her right hand of painted fingernails into the cup of water and allowed only a drop or two of water to roll off her fingers and into the vial. She repeated this process a few times until there was the perfect mixture in the vial. Then she quickly grabbed the rag that was in the shoebox to dry both her hand and the vial.

Arm-and-Hammer baking soda was the next thing she pulled from the shoebox and added a pinch to the vial. After she tore matches in pairs, to the tune of a dozen or so sets, I realized the process was complete and we were ready for action.

Lindor was in a zone. She took a deep breath and then picked up a pair of matches. There was a striker pad taped to the TV dinner tray. The sound of the matches touching upon the striker was distinct. The sound of friction with the slow drag across the plate caught my ear, as I waited for that undeniable pop that produced a flame and captivated me with its glow.

Lindor slowly brought the flame and the vial together, keeping a certain distance between the two. Her gaze intensified as she peered into what looked like a vial filled with skim milk. Whatever she was searching for was somewhere in the midst of that milky mess.

She began to slowly spin the vial, swirling its contents. By this time, I noticed the flame of the match was burning down close to her fingertips. Not alarmed, she dropped the lit match onto the ashtray and, without missing a beat, grabbed another pair of matches off the table. She was able to light them off the previous pair and proceeded forward. This was all done while never removing her eyes from the prize.

I was spellbound as I watched this mixture come to a slow boil, and for as long as it took the process to get to this point, it switched gears twice as fast.

All of a sudden, her movements changed and she quickly threw the match onto the ashtray while she reached for another pinch of baking soda and dropped it into the vial. This procedure caused everything in the vial to foam towards the top and it appeared as if it was about to spill over.

However, Lindor had everything under control. She dipped her fingers back into the cool water and placed drops in the vial again and again until a light, yellowish-beige colored gel began to form at the bottom of the vial. She continued to add more drops of water and then placed a broken wire from a coat hanger into the vial. I had no idea what this was all about, but within a few seconds the gel started to change colors as it seemed to harden.

She quickly stirred the hanger around in circles until the gel was rock hard. Without warning, a huge, satisfied smile showed up on her face. She removed this chunky, hard, white substance from the vial and began to blow on it. I was taken aback by the attention and care that was given to this rock. It was almost as if this rock was a god.

After it was dry, she placed it onto a broken mirror and used a razor to chop off a piece. She took a deep breath, picked up her bricker brack glass pipe and placed the piece of the cocaine rock on one end. The cooked coke, crack, or whatever else it was labeled, sat high on its perch above a bunch of matted down circular wire screens, similar to the ones you would remove from your kitchen sink faucet. Lindor was efficient and we were about to indulge!

She took one single match this time and lit it. With her left hand, she gently raised the glass pipe and crack to head level as she sat up straight with perfect posture. Trust me, the portrait of Mona Lisa had nothing on Lindor's pose. It was beautiful.

She licked her full, ruby red lips and placed them around the glass stem that extended from the body of the pipe. Simultaneously, she lowered the flame with her right hand towards the rock. I noticed the flame would drop onto the rock causing the sounds of snap, crackle and pop - just like when milk hits a bowl of Rice Krispies cereal.

I waited for her reaction and there was none. The only thing she did was put the match out and place it into the ashtray. The white rock that once sat on its perch had disappeared; melted away. Then I realized that the coke must not have been good. I started to apologize about scoring some garbage and I was prepared to spend more cash to get her something real when she stuck her hand out to silence me. She was not through.

Lindor took another deep breath and this time she let out a relaxing sigh. She went back into her upright pose, only this time she stood up at the edge of the bed lighting a pair of matches and setting the pipe ablaze. The glass pipe quickly filled up with smoke and I saw a white cloud that streamed from the pipe stack, almost like a choo-choo train.

Her luscious lips embraced the stem as she slowly inhaled the white cloud. Like a Rolex time piece, her movements were calculated as she slowly spun the pipe clockwise from the twelve o'clock upright position to the three o'clock sideways position, and finally, to the six o'clock upside down position. She held onto the matches to the point where the flames had nothing else to burn except her finger. What was crazy to me was that she had no reaction from the flame burning her finger. It seemed to have no effect on her, and when she was done, she simply placed what was left of the matches in the ashtray.

I should have run from the room, but I ignored conventional wisdom, common sense, mother's wit and that small voice that was always with me and I stayed put. The room had a smell of sulfur and the presence of something disturbing in the air.

I continued to watch her every move as she sat the pipe down and placed her right index finger and thumb on her nose and pinched her nostrils together. It seemed as if she was trying to force air out of her while keeping it all locked in. I say it like this, because I watched her cheeks swell up with air, but she would not release all the smoke that she just took in.

She held onto this hit for what seemed to be a solid 30 seconds until…Lindor, the fire-breathing dragon, let loose! A cloud of thick white smoke filled the room and I witnessed Lindor's transform. Suddenly beads of sweat appeared on her brow as if she had run through a sprinkler system. Her eyes became cold and she was able to look directly through me as if I was not in the room.

She slowly began to move around, I watched her peer

down the hallway for a moment, and then she scanned the room. Her eyes locked on her bedroom window. She walked over and, from a distance, peeked through her blinds. After a few minutes of this, she turned and looked at the TV table with all of the items scattered over it. In a panic, she started to clean up everything, placing the glass pipe and the coke on her person and quickly placing everything else in her shoe box.

She had the look. I recognized the same zombie appearance from the time Marvin and I were in California visiting his contact. I am sure the expression on my face was saying something; I was puzzled as to how and why people do this to themselves.

Then, ten minutes later, as if nothing transpired, she snapped out of it and smiled. She began to talk to me, assuring me that she was fine. Well, it was not her I was worrying about. She went on to tell me that she was not crazy. If I did not know better from the past experience with Marvin, I would have thought so, and if she was not crazy, maybe I was for being there.

She left the room and returned wearing a different see through night gown. Okay, now I was starting to put the pieces of the puzzle together. My selfish desires kicked in and the question "What's in it for me?" arose. Any answer was about to be addressed and there was a silver lining after all. As we sat back on the bed, we began to embrace and she hit me with a background probing question.

"What kind of drugs have you tried before?" Well, the Ronald James ego was not about to sound like a novice, so I listed everything except smoking coke. She then asked a more pointed question, "Have you ever smoked the pipe?" I told her yes and explained that I tried it once, but it never did anything for me. I had no idea why I was engaging in this conversation; it could only lead me to troubles.

Her next question came straight from the pages of Genesis Chapter 3. 'Do you want to try some fruit of the tree of knowledge of good and evil? Ye shall not surely die.' She went on to justify…"Ron, look at all the other drugs you have tried and you were okay. Don't you just want to try a small hit?" STOP IT WOMAN! Are you out of your freaking mind? I know the story, oh, but man-pride got in the way. Besides, if Adam could blame the woman, why couldn't I?

I would have to say this single event, coupled with every other event that lead me to this point, would cost me at least 20 years of my life. I kept saying to myself, "Ron, all you have to do is say no…just say NO!" That did not happen and I said "Yes."

Lindor sat up and moved so fast that I never saw it coming. She had everything back out on the TV tray, plus the glass pipe with a piece of crack cocaine in its perch headed toward my mouth like a mothers nipple. I moved awkwardly as I tried to hold the pipe. Lindor was a professional and noticed my inexperience and regained control. I was told to relax she was in the driver's seat and held the pipe, lit the matches and instructed me on what to do next.

I was told to pull very slowly as I inhaled. I was doing fine and then she stopped me and told me to blow out the smoke. When I did, I noticed there was not much and I did not notice anything different in the way I felt. This was just like my last experience with this stuff. She told me again to catch my breath and relax.

I was instructed to draw off the pipe very slow, only this time I could feel the cool white cloud entering my very being. As she spun the pipe clockwise, I was told to pull until I could not suck in anything else. I held this for what felt like forever and when I finally exhaled, I believe smoke came out of every hole in my body.

Instantaneously, every bell, whistle, siren and drum went off in my head and I broke out into a cold sweat with my heart racing. I was in love! I had just had an encounter with my future wife: "Maggie Mae".

My whole experience with crack cocaine is summed up in the lyrics of *Maggie Mae*, one of the popular songs by the great music artist, Rod Stewart. 'Maggie I couldn't have tried any harder; wrecked my bed, kicked me in the head; you stole my heart. I couldn't leave you if I tried. You made a first class fool out of me. Maggie, I wish I never saw your face. I'll get on home one of these days.'

I want you to know I was turned on…and then turned out on crack. Crack/Maggie Mae, Maggie Mae/Crack became my life, my love, my everything. Rod must have known something about love to have written that song. In my eyes, crack cocaine and Maggie Mae were synonymous with each other.

I believe everyone comes to some sort of cross roads in life, whether it means serving self, alcohol, work, drugs, lust, power, greed, money or Maggie Mae. Something or someone you love or lust after and everyone is tempted to leave home for it. Rod, thanks for the heads up, but I did not pay enough attention to the words in your song.

I stood there with my mind questioning my mind. My natural senses were on high alert, heightened as if I was in tune with another world. I must have been completely out of it for at least 10 minutes…what a rush! This was living life on the edge and this is how I wanted to continue living!

Slowly, I began to hear this whisper that seemed to be in the distance, but it was not clear. Then the voice become clearer and louder and it almost sounded familiar, like someone I knew. It sounded like Lindor's voice…"Ron-Ron." I heard my name being called over and over again. "Ron-Ron." Was this Lindor chanting my college nickname? How did she know my nickname? Then I started begging for an explanation, "What is happening to me?"

Before I could go on full tilt, I heard Lindor say to me, "Ron, are you alright?" My eyes and ears became focused and the ringing bells stopped, but my heart and mind were still racing a mile a minute. Oh no way, I just became one of them…a crack zombie! The crazy part about me getting hooked on crack was that with each experience after that I wanted to reach that same high point, feeling the exact same rush I felt when getting high with Lindor. I spent years chasing after that high, but it never was the same pure madness.

So now, back to reality of life with Gypsy, creating the cleaning company, moving out of state – only now I had the added desire of getting high on crack. It's amazing how much time you miss when you are high!

After collecting our insurance money from the fake accident and setting The Jugs on fire, we moved our family out to Wichita, Kansas. My two cousins, Peanut and Paul, welcomed us with open arms. It took only a hot minute to gain employment. I started selling cars, plus our janitorial business was up and running too. We purchased a very nice home in the quiet side of town and I thought all was well with our world. However, just as fast as we settled in, I ran into a major problem.

As hard as I tried, I could not end the madness of alcohol, women and Maggie Mae. Everything I worked for, lied for or stole to achieve was now subject to go up in smoke, literally. I mean everything, including my recent marriage to Cheryl, the

Jets Janitorial Business, my best friend and frat brother, plus countless business relationships, jobs, friends and family. All were subject to be lost.

I did everything in my own power to hold things together…well, looking back, not everything. I could have sought professional help to stop what I was doing – the thought had crossed my mind a few times, but it was clouded by the smoke! So, in order for me to keep feeding my habit, I would need more money. However, it was money that I did not have, so yours truly came up with a grand plan to put us back on top. We were about to be robbed.

My plan was that I would stage a burglary to our home and file a claim against our own insurance company. That is exactly what I did, too. One evening, we all went out to the movies, but prior to us leaving, I stashed a number of high quality items out of sight and then ransacked our home, breaking a door and window on the side of our house on my way out.

After returning from the movies, I dialed 911 and the fun began. The police responded to the call, followed by a detective who had a number of questions, followed by photos taken of our home, and lastly, a complete dusting for fingerprints. There I stood, yours truly, a full-fledged criminal making sure my story was sound because none of us wanted to go to jail, especially me, myself and I.

So as the man of the house, I stepped up and sealed the deal with the detective. I could not stand another question. I performed and deserved an Oscar for my role. The award should have been more like a stiff prison sentence; however, things worked out and we called in our claims the following day.

After making our claim, I found out something about the

average Joe business man. When it came to their integrity with insurance policies and customers who needed to file claims, they were willing to outright lie. Yes, they know that whatever was placed on paper and presented to the insurance company would later result in cash for them. This happened across the board from electronics to jewelry and I played right into their greed. I was able to work a deal with one of the jewelry stores to accept an insurance check for a gold nugget watch that had been 'stolen' in exchange for cash.

Things were so easy as far as making claims and collecting money from the insurance company that it gave me another idea. Since I was smoking things up as fast as the money came in, I decided to go back to the well for a second time. I claimed that some other items were missing, overlooked from the first list, so the insurance company processed and paid me for them as well.

Now there I was – smoked out of my mind – broke, without a job and faced with all kinds of other family issues and court problems that I neglected to resolve. Our bills were behind, forged checks had been written all around town and they were bouncing left and right, and worst of all, I had no sense of direction other than I wanted another hit.

The genius in me was very active when it came to ways of self-satisfaction and I had come up with yet another brilliant idea...why not sell some of our stuff that was stashed from the fake break-in, that we already received money for from the insurance company?! Hey, they were reported stolen anyway and the yard was big enough so why not have an 'Everything Must Go Sale'?

The 10-speed bikes, fish tank, computer, big screen TV, tools, washer and dryer, Cheryl's knick-knacks, art work and so on. We set up our next door neighbor with brand new monster mudders for his 4-wheel drive truck. We wrote checks and more checks to get cash. Again, as fast as the money came in, it was smoked up.

Cheryl was fed up with this type of lifestyle and wanted it to stop. This created a conflict between us because I was just getting started. However, the next bump in the road came when my inner voice told me we were sitting ducks from too much of a paper trail we had created in Kansas.

It was time to pack up and head back to Philly. We had another yard sale, only this time both Cheryl and I were on the same page. It was time to get out of Wichita. There were no good-byes and we did not provide any explanations to our neighbors. We just rented a U-Haul truck, loaded what was left of our belongings and we were off to Philadelphia.

When we reached Philly, we moved in with some of Cheryl's family, but I was not happy because I wanted to continue to get high. My wife, on the other hand, was ready to move on with or without me, so I searched for females to get high with…but not just any females. I yearned for crack smoking females. For some reason, I was able to easily approach these women who smoked crack because they wanted money or crack and I wanted sex. I gave them what they wanted and I ended up getting tricked, conned, put-out, gamed, jumped and sometimes, if I was lucky, sex.

Let me speak on this for a moment and this message is for all you single ladies and men out there. The education course called Trick 101 is not what you think. This course is for men, and women designed it. The average male, with or without drugs, is subject to the game. He meets a girl, she smiles and all seems innocent enough. However, the game is well underway and the female is asked out on a date. Money is spent on cards, flowers, dinner, a movie, hotel, etc…you get the picture.

Some men would stop me here because they say the girls today are the ones that buy them the clothes, take them out and pay for their dinner. This is the female's new spin on the old game. I say the old game was that if the man did all those things for her, she opened her legs to you. Then you were dancing to her tune no matter who paid for dinner.

Female needs are affection, companionship, safety and then financial security, with an open mind and all the honesty in the world. If she is paying for you to be with her, it is only about sex and you just got tricked. It is obvious she does not need your money and once she pulls back on any of those things she had been providing for you, we will see who will be chasing whom.

I will tell you that things get even more clouded when drugs are involved. The crack tells me that I want sex; however, I cannot even function once it is in my system. When I get high, I belong totally to Maggie Mae.

The rest of this chapter is very difficult for me to place in chronological order because events are unclear due to my life moving so fast, and I was always on some kind of drug. However and without question, each and every day seemed to contain an event of some significance. From October 1988 when I landed back in Philly with Cheryl to October 1990, I would have to say unequivocally, it was the most dangerous time in my life.

Let me tell you folks, I was living at the epicenter of pure madness. I left the mid-west and found myself in the wild, wild, west smack dab in Southwest Philly. I have had over 20 separate occasions where either guns were pointed directly at me, cracked square upside my head, stuffed down my throat or discharged in my direction with intentions of blowing my brains out…not to mention the fights, the beat downs, the knives, the boards and the baseball bats that gravitated towards me. Yes, these were very dangerous times in my life. On the other hand, I also know that these times were blessed.

In the shadows and the unseen, God, with His untold love, grace and mercy towards me, had orchestrated a heavenly host of angels with the sole mission of keeping me alive. It was clear that my only mission was to get high when everything around me spelled death. Why was my life spared? What did the big guy in the sky want with me?

These questions and many others circulated in my mind, but none so profound that it led me to stop what I was doing. What was made known to me were my mother's cries and prayers, and the prayers of my godmother, aunts, grandmother, family members, friends and even strangers who saw me in a state way beyond what I could see myself. For the sake of our tree forest, I will share just a few stories of why people were praying for me.

Southwest Philly was a crack house haven and, within a two-block radius anywhere in the neighborhood, there were close to 20 houses available to get high. What qualified the place to be labeled a crack house? It was simple…Frequent and repeat crack heads into a house that was 'open' twenty-four hours a day, seven days a week and where anything goes. What was the reason I said 'anything goes'? Because anything went - fights, stick ups, stabbings, shootings, murder, orgies, sex, people hiding out, people planning, plotting, scheming, scamming and conniving…not to mention smoking crack! Believe it or not, when I was not at my mother's house, these were the places I called home, but never did I think of myself as a crack head…not Ron James!

The crack head is constantly high and spends hours in a zombie mode with a much distorted view of the surrounding world. They are what are called the "Schitz", short for schizophrenia. The schitz was tailor made for this type of lifestyle and I have witnessed, even have been part of, the experiences that accompany crack head schizophrenia.

It can have a person hide in closets or stand still motionless for untold amounts of time, have fits of tearing a room apart looking for nothing, uncontrollable body movements, self-mutilation, digging in pockets for something when nothing is there, or undressing others or themselves and running around the streets without a care in the world.

I have even seen people pull out all types of guns and weapons, and some have even jumped out of windows. I say these things only because once a house becomes available to crack, the crack heads soon follow…and the problems with crack heads are that they are unpredictable.

The crack house can be an abandoned, run down house that has been boarded up by the city with no utilities unless someone illegally hooks them up, which is not uncommon. Everything from rats to roaches to dead bodies would be found inside. The smell would be so strong it would knock you out cold, unless you were in zombie mode. Sometimes I discovered that smell actually coming from me, as I would go for days without washing. I was quite offensive, even to myself, as if I had lost all sense of pride, but for the sake of what?

On the flip side, I have been in some crack houses that are run as tight as a prison where someone of authority oversees the entire operation. You are led inside, escorted to a paid room where they provide everything from coke to women, and no one is allowed to mess with you. When your money is gone, so are you. The events of the house changed as each individual entered, but the one component of crack remained constant.

Because I kept moving from house to house, I found myself meeting many different people. I stumbled upon a unique trio – two guys and a girl – who were go-getters and called themselves "clockers". Why? Twenty-four hours a day, seven days a week, at any given place, they were able to get cash. However, do not mistake them for the drug dealer who stands on the corner selling drugs. What this crew did was use their creative abilities to sell themselves.

The three of them would venture off to high traffic intersections and park their car alongside the road. Once the car was in place, it became a prop. The car's hood was lifted up and they would move into action. One of the guys would partner up with the girl and head in one direction, and the other guy would head in another direction.

The game went something like this: The clocker would approach the victim whether at a traffic light, intersection, stop sign, parking lot, shopping mall or anywhere you could find people. The clocker would then share a story of their car being broken down and needing additional cash for repairs. They were counting on the victim handing over money. Their story may have gone something like this:

Clocker:	Excuse me Sir/Ma'am, my car has broken down and I am trying to get to work. Can you help me please?
Victim:	What is wrong?
Clocker:	My fan belt is shot and I only have $16. I need $14 to repair it.
Victim:	Excuse me?
Clocker:	I need $14 more to get a new fan belt. Could

	you please help me? If you give me your name and number, or business card, I can repay you.
Victim:	Oh, that is not necessary. Here is $20 and I hope you make out all right.

This scam was simple, to the point, and after twenty minutes of time, this trio was back in their own car on their way to the cop man to buy crack. Sometimes they would put all their money together in order to purchase enough crack to hold them down for most of the night. However, almost always they purchased caps, so within the hour they were out of crack and out the door again.

Clocking went on twenty-four seven and you could not help but get involved with it. When I came over to their spot, I would share an obscene amount of crack with them, so eventually they invited me on a few clocking runs with them.

It only took me a hot second to catch on and perfect my game and when I did, I took it to another level. Often dressed in a shirt and tie or suit, I played the same game, but with a new twist:

Me:	Excuse me sir/ma'am, "Please forgive me, my wife and I are broken down. Our car is right here.
Victim:	What's wrong?
Me:	We are broken down and we cannot get home. The tow truck wants $83.50, our AAA just expired, and my wife is giving me a hard time because I forgot to renew it.
Victim:	What do you need?
Me:	I have $49 on me and I need $34.50 more to get towed (but most of the time, I did not have a dime on me).

Victim:	Where do you live?
Me:	I was from anywhere I needed to be – usually pulling out a recently collected business card from someone I just met or from a store fishbowl collecting cards for a contest. "Listen, if you can help me I will give you my license and registration…as a matter of fact, please take my wife, she's driving me crazy." NOTE: if they laughed, smiled or gave some type of positive motion, I knew I was going to get something.
Victim:	Here is $30, $40 or sometimes $50.

I have received as much as $300 from one person doing this scam, not to mention hitting three to five victims at a time for $30 - $50 each, which was not bad for twenty minutes worth of work. Now, I am not glorifying this lifestyle or any scam for that matter. I really believe the average person truly was out to help me by doing a charitable deed, plus this scam and others were not all fun and games.

Murphy's Law would sometimes rain down on me and I would find myself in front of the same person who gave me money a few days ago and was not as kind the second time around. People have chased me on foot and in cars.

One time a guy gave me his last $40, but when he realized what I was up to, he came back for his money with a vengeance. He tried to take my head off with a baseball bat and he left me alone only after I threw his money back at him.

On two separate occasions, I had people pull guns on me as I approached their vehicles, and other times I had been chased and locked up by the police. What clocking did was provide me with a way to gain money for my addiction at any given time. When I look back on this, I am ashamed because part of my tactic was to prey on the weak and yet I never hesitated to tell someone I was a Christian.

On March 3, 1989, I was locked up by the Springfield Township Police Department for theft by deception, bad checks and disorderly conduct. The prison looked just like an old castle and it reminded me of the Norristown Jail where I had previously served time. Somehow, Cheryl came to my rescue, hired a lawyer, and I ended up doing only three months.

However, during this time, something slowly started to change in me. I had entered the jail physically, emotionally and spiritually run down, and after spending a few days in Intake, I was finally taken to B block and placed in a cell with a guy from New York City. When you move into someone's cell, jailhouse policy dictates he has the advantage by having time in and you have to follow his rules until you can establish your own. This was the case with me, and my new cellmate was in charge because of the time he already had in.

He had everything that someone could want while serving time, plus he had prison clout and the respect of everyone. So when I came through the door with nothing except my run over sneakers, which were not allowed in his cell, I felt somewhat at a disadvantage. I was not getting good vibes from this arrangement; I had no other choice but to stick it out. Then, for whatever reason, when I came back from the Counselor's office later that day I found out I had been moved to a cell with a guy who was mentally challenged. I can only say that it was once again the angels keeping me out of harm's way.

During my stay at Delaware County Prison, I found myself wandering around the block looking for somewhere to land

and, to my surprise, I found Jesus. Well, I ran smack into Him and His love through a bunch of men who were having Bible study. One of the guys shared his time by helping me read the Bible; he was such an encouragement.

One day during Bible study, he pushed me to read God's word in front of everyone. I was scared to try because all the thoughts from fourth grade immediately rushed in, but I did it anyway…and just like I thought, I messed up big time! However, this time no one laughed or made any smart comments. Instead, all I received were pats on the back for stepping forward….it was nothing like I thought.

This guy also asked to be moved into my cell and then challenged me to read a book called *Prison to Praise*. This was the first book I read from cover to cover in my entire life. I was on top of the world! Spiritually, I felt like I was growing. I was going to Bible studies, church, reading God's word and even praying. Before I knew it, my time at Delaware County Prison was over and I was ready to test my faith out in the world.

With a hug from my new friend and my Bible in hand, I was sent back into the wild, wild world of Southwest Philly. It took me only half of a day to pick up where I had left off. Pure madness! I put my Bible down and picked up Maggie Mae… With all that said, let us begin my stories of the pure madness that was my life, even after having experienced prison life.

The first story takes place on 60th and Kingssion Avenue about ten o'clock at night and I had just gotten my hands on forty dollars – this was going to be a good first blast of the day. I went to cop from a guy who was serving jumbo caps, which were supposed to be "the bomb" on the streets now. Jumbo caps were small, clear plastic capsules that were two inches in length and gave the illusion of getting more, but it actually had crack crumbs, not rocks, for contents. It was just another method of making money off crack heads, and obviously, it was working.

When I got to his house, I gave him my money and was told to wait a few minutes as he was still in the process of repackaging. Well, standing outside of his house on that corner, acting as if I were waiting for a trolley car, was not the thing to do. That corner was made for people who really needed the bus or trolley, and before I knew it, one was pulling up to drop people off.

A guy stepped off and I recognized him as someone who had often turned me on to a free high. I was glad to see him, I asked him how he had been, and he asked me what I was doing in that part of town. I shared that I was waiting for my delivery, so he wanted to know if could he get down with me and was excited when I told him yes.

We were still waiting for my delivery and I began to tell him about the jumbo caps and the quality of this product when all of the sudden, out of the shadows of the night, appeared four young bucks in their early twenties crossing the street. As they came closer, I looked at their faces, but did not recognize any of them; however, I could not say the same for my home boy.

Everyone made eye contact and my home boy got nervous really fast. As all this was going on, I noticed that the "leader" was drinking a forty-ounce bottle of beer. He stopped the group to have a serious discussion with them, and I knew then that something was wrong.

They passed us, headed down the street, but quickly doubled backed and came right up to my boy and said, "Hey old head, weren't you the one who picked up our packs the other day when Five-O ran up on our corner?" I looked at him, then at the boys who were waiting for a response, and then back at my boy. He replied, "No, no, that was not me. It was my cousin and we look a lot alike."

Again, they walked off and my inside voice told me to leave now, but I shot it down because I had a hot date with Maggie Mae. Besides, the guy I was copping from was due to show up any second with the delivery. I did have enough sense to ask my boy if everything was all right and he reassured me all was well, so I told him to meet me around the corner.

Before I could let that thought settle in my mind, the leader boy was back with his forty-ounce bottle and he stood one foot in front of my boy and said to him, "No, I think that was you". He then raised the half-full bottle of beer high in the air as he guzzled down what remained. I thought to myself, "This cannot be good!"

As the last drop was sucked past his lips, he took the empty bottle and smashed it at our feet and then he sucker punched my homeboy! Aw, man! Home boy stumbled and stepped back against a parked car and before I could really come to terms with what just happened, these bucks were stomping him out! I went into my Good Samaritan mode, grabbed one of the bucks with each hand, and pulled them off and away from my boy. Big mistake on my part!

When I did this it never occurred to me what would happen next. My boy sprang to his feet and saw just enough daylight to make an exit – he took off like a bolt of lightning, leaving me there with four very disturbed young guys looking for recreation. All their anger and energy was now focused on you know who…yep, Mr. Good Samaritan! So much for wanting to help someone. Oh damn, here it comes!

I took a blow to my face and saw that flash of light that comes from a sucker punch, and then took a few blows to the back of my head. My fists went into action, but I was unable to make solid connections on any of my targets because I was in somewhat of a daze. Then I heard the voice of the guy who was to deliver my crack and he yelled out, "What the hell is up?" Surely, he was going to help me out, like one Good Samaritan to another…

FAT CHANCE! I guess he felt an adult taking punches at kids was not the best situation and he decided he needed to help them instead of me, so now it was five-to-one. If things could not have gotten any worse, a carload of boys stopped in the middle of the street to help the guys who were fighting me. Well nine-to-one was not working for me and I knew I had to make a swift getaway…and make it fast!

I was able to knock one of the boys out cold and that gave me the break I needed, so I took off. No sooner had I gotten away when one of the bucks yelled out for me to stop. Well, I was never good at following directions and I was not about to start now. I began running faster and as I glanced back, I saw a gun drawn, so my adrenaline kicked in and my body could barely keep up with my feet. I made it around the corner and up the next street to my safe house, only to find my homeboy standing there. *Are you serious?!*

As I stood there panting for air with blood running down the side of my face, he only had one question for me, "Did you get the crack?" I felt like giving him a little bit of what I just went through!

My second story…I had personal checks left over from the state of Kansas, so with paper to burn, I decided to use them up with any and everyone who would accept them. One day I put my game face on and walked boldly into a new women's clothing and apparel store where I just happened to have met the owner. I knew from the start he wanted to sell me everything he could; I was willing to accommodate him. I told him I needed to make up with my wife and thought I would surprise her with a few outfits.

That was a bold face lie since the sizes I was providing him belonged to someone other than my wife...and man, was she gonna be fly! He walked me all around the store and presented different outfits, styles, combinations, looks and colors. After a great conversation, the items selected were placed on the counter and the total rang up to a whopping sixteen-hundred dollars.

Without hesitation, I pulled out my trusty checkbook and pen and went to work. I presented the owner with a check from Mr. James of Wichita, Kansas, and just like that, I left the store with my arms full of women's clothing...Sweet! The getting was so good that I tried my hand at it a second time two days later to the tune of three-hundred dollars.

Now everyone that has ever been involved in Crime101 class knows that a criminal is not supposed to return to the scene of the crime, but nine times out of ten they always do and end up getting busted. So who in their right mind would try this store a third time? Me! Incorrigible me! That's who! What in the world would make me even try? *Are you serious?!* Well, Maggie Mae, of course.

On my third visit, I had a new twist and that was a payroll check printed out for $600. The owner was not there and a young black woman was working the store that day. I quickly ran around the store and placed a number of items on the counter. I felt this was a great opportunity because the owner was not in and I thought I could play this girl since she seemed to be green around the edges.

I was going back and forth with her as to why she should accept my check, but she remained firm in restating the store's policy numerous times over. I told her about how I knew the owner and my past shopping experiences. Still, she stood firm on her declaration, "Sir I am sorry, but our store does not accept checks." I responded, "Well, why don't you call the owner and I am sure he will tell you differently."

To my surprise, she picked up the phone and dialed away. Not knowing how I would be received on the other end, I looked at the front door just in case I needed to make a clean getaway. She began to engage in a conversation with the owner and I quickly had to take control, so I demanded to speak with him. She passed the phone to me and I went to work on him.

I told him my wife was so pleased with the previous items that I wanted to come back to pick up a few pieces for her mother. The owner was sold and I gave the phone back to the young woman. The owner addressed the issue and that was that. I had failed to mention the one minor detail to the owner that it was a payroll check and not a personal check… gosh, it must have slipped my mind!

As the young woman rang up the sale, she apologized for giving me such a hard time. The sale totaled two hundred dollars and all she needed to do was hand over my change. However, when she went into the register drawer, she could only come up with about one-hundred dollars and some change…Houston, we have a problem! I told her that I would take the items and the one-hundred dollars and I could return for the rest of my change later.

She cut me off saying, "No, I have an idea." Then she went into her own money and made up the difference stating, "The owner can repay me when he comes back later in the afternoon." I left the store a very happy man with all the clothes and four-hundred dollars in cash!

Well, several days later with the money spent, I found

myself walking aimlessly through the streets of West Philly. I would say I was about four blocks away from that same women's dress store and the only thing on my mind was my next high.

My focus was somewhat interrupted when that familiar small voice quietly said, "Look behind you." When I did, the only thing I saw from the corner of my eye was a small black hatchback slowly driving away. As I continued walking, I felt things were a little unusual, but not enough to alarm me and I kept walking towards the center of the street.

As my gaze followed the lines of the street, I once again noticed that same black hatchback now parked in the middle of the street about two blocks down. I thought it was someone who was lost and needed directions, but as I got closer, the car sped off. Okay, now I knew something was wrong.

I directed my attention to who was in that car and seemingly what did they want with me. Everything was made very clear a few second later when the black hatchback came zooming down the street with its tires coming to a screeching halt about twenty feet from me.

The doors flew open and from within the confines of that small black car emerged two enraged individuals! Both were wearing black gloves, one carried a long crow bar and the other carried chains. I quickly focused on the driver, but had never seen this guy before in my life, so I shifted my eyes to the passenger, and holy crap…it was the dress store owner! He was not his friendly self, and it was very clear these guys meant business. Once again, God gets the credit for what happened next!

When I turned around to start my run in the opposite direction, out of nowhere appeared an older man in his late 60's who just got out of a station wagon. He was two feet in front of me and the only thing I had time to say before these guys got their hands on me was, "Sir, please help me – they are trying to kill me!"

He did not question me, he did not ignore me. He was one of God's angels who stopped only a split second to look back and see the two men coming at me. He turned back towards me and said with haste, "Get in the car!" It was apparent that I was not moving fast enough and the next thing I knew, this angel gripped me off my feet with both his hands and literally flung me through the driver's side open door into the passenger's seat.

He jumped in behind the wheel and we took off, caught up in a high-speed chase that lasted for several blocks. He knew the streets better than I did and after turns I could not even tell you we made, the chase finally ended; mercy prevailed. When I got out of his car, my knees shaking from the experience, I thanked him over and over again, yet all he did was laugh that we got out of that one alive...*Are you serious?!*

If the stories up until now have not proved that I lacked sound judgment to stay out of trouble, the next story begs the question 'Did you not have any sense at all?' and goes something like this:

I had been running wild for days at a time. Most of my cash had been spent with Jamaicans on Upland Street in Southwest Philly, just around the corner from where Cheryl's oldest daughter lived. I was in and out of her house for safety and then back to the Jamaicans, dropping close to two-hundred dollars every time I went there. They saw me as a research animal hooked on their bait because I had spent an untold amount of cash at their place. However, all good runs must come to an end...and this one almost came to a dead end.

For years, both of Cheryl's daughters put up with my madness, often begging me to slow down or stop so I would not be killed or kill myself. Even though Cheryl had moved on from our marriage, the girls never stopped loving me and I was grateful to have them still care about me.

It was around two o'clock in the morning when I walked back out into the street from one of the daughter's house. All I could think about was having just one more blast and then I would take it down…and, by now, you have realized that was never going to happen! One hit is too many and a million hits will never be enough.

The word 'crack head' was demeaning. I never liked it and I never used it, but that did not stop people from using the term. Therefore, as I walked down the street towards the Jamaicans, a car drove by me and from inside someone yelled, "Hey you, crack head!" I turned around to see to whom they were talking, hoping I could get a hit from that person, but no one was around except me. When I looked back at the car, I realized they were talking about me, to me. I had spent many, many hours in the crack house located next to the daughter's house and, this night being no exception, found myself always looking for my next hit, but I never considered myself a crack head…not until that moment.

All I had in my pocket was one dollar and seventy-five cents; that would not buy anything on the streets, let alone at a dealer. Although, I figured the Jamaicans would spot me one last time, so I went over to see if I could at least get a five-dollar cap on the I.O.U. I knew I would be good for it because of all the money I had already spent with them.

Well, in the drug world, some will work with you and some will not. In this case, I was sadly mistaken to think the Jamaicans were willing to work with me. He told me in no uncertain terms did they spot a cap or issue an I.O.U...it was either a money deal or no deal and to get off the damn porch. However, I was persistent and explained I had just spent thousands of dollars in their house over the past few days; all I needed were a few caps on credit.

He had little compassion, but gave me a ray of hope when he said he would work with me if I could come up with some cash. Well, that was music to my ears so I set off with my $1.75 and shot back around the corner in hopes to find a few more dollars. I was totally exhausted, but instead of calling it quits, I pressed the streets. I tried clocking, but this particular night it did not work at all. I felt defeated and headed for the safety of Cheryl's daughter's house.

When I got back to her block, I ran smack into one of my crack head junkies. He was back in the neighborhood and the kind of person who was down for anything – fights, stickups, whatever. This guy was an 'anything goes' type of dude, but by no means was he a sucker, and he always knew how to get his hands on a few dollars.

As soon as I saw him, I told him what the Jamaican guy said and asked if he had any money. He was already half wasted, but his eyes lit up and he said, "Yes!", so I stuck my hand out to get the cash...only to find out what he had was a handful of pennies. I thought to myself, "Are you serious?! Pennies!" Well, he had pennies, a nickel and a dime, mixed with a few lint balls, so my best guess was that it amounted to $ .32. I should have asked the both of us how much sense we really had and then taken my black ass inside, called it a night, and crashed.

Well, that would not have made for an exciting story, now would it? I accepted the change from him and placed it all inside the dollar bill, lint balls included, and the two of us hustled around the corner to the cop spot.

With money in hand, I took the lead and went up on the porch. After knocking and knocking, the Jamaican finally came to the mail slot and I told him I had more money and then stuffed the bill containing the change into the slot.

The next thing I heard was the guy cursing me out in his native tongue as the change hit the floor. It sounded like the change went in all directions and he called me all kinds of names. I stood there for the next ten minutes or so trying to talk this guy into giving me at least two $5 caps. He was not going for it, so I then tried talking him into giving me my money back. Are you serious? Asking for money back from a dealer! Man, what was I smokin'?

We were at a stale mate…or so I thought. He told me to wait a minute and disappeared from the door. I thought I had won. When he came back to the slot, he passed me a cap. All was well until I looked at its contents in the street light. This guy had taken most of the crack out of the cap. It was useless for me to go back on the porch and argue any further, so I walked to the corner to locate my partner, but to my surprise, he was nowhere in sight.

I had two distinct thoughts about why he bailed on me – one, he must have run into someone else who had crack in hand, or two, being in his crack head state of mind, he went on another mission, forgetting about me. Oh well, there was only enough for one-half of a hit anyway, so I took what I thought would be my last blast for that night. After I hit the pipe, my energy level was restored and I found myself out again searching for another hit. Would this craziness ever end?!

I recall walking up the center of the street when in the distance I heard a very familiar voice yelling, "Daddy Ron, watch out!" No sooner had I turned my head towards the sound of that voice when I was struck from behind with a 2 x

4 board. Once again, God's mercy saved me from some very damaging injuries, if not death.

Immediately after the hit, I tried to make sense of a thirty-two cent situation. I was able to keep from falling, but stumbled backwards about a yard, which gave me just enough time to focus on who had hit me. There stood the unhappy acquaintance who had given me his thirty-two cents, winding up for a second hit! What the hell was going on?!

With what sense I had left, I was able to grab the board as he swung, but the damage was already done. My left eye was completely swollen shut and I had only partial vision from my right eye. Blood ran out of my face; I was in bad shape. After grabbing the board, I was able to square off with him, and he ended up running away.

For thirty-two cents, I got the sense knocked out of me! The next time I saw him in the neighborhood, he pulled a gun on me and said he did not want any more trouble…I was the one who took the brunt of the trouble the last time, so I certainly did not want any more of what he was dishing out. Both of us had plenty of sense that day to leave well enough alone. *Are you serious?!*

This fourth story takes place during a time when very few people wanted anything to do with me, including my family. I had been running the streets of North Philly and, for whatever reason, I decided to run across town to Cheryl's daughter's place in Southwest Philly.

My only problems: it was late, I had no ride, and I had no cash. I had, though, been able to score an icy cold forty-ounce beer before the bars closed, so I cracked the seal and turned it up – alcohol seemed to level me off. With twenty dollars worth of crack in my pocket and an icy cold one in my hand,

I began to walk off my high. That was when I spotted a cab and, out of instinct, my hand shot up in the air for his view.

He passed by slowly to investigate this possible fare; he must not have liked what he saw because he kept driving past me. Then I saw him peering at me in his rearview mirror, so I threw my arms into the air as if I was frustrated that he did not stop. The brake lights flashed as he came to a stop and put the car in reverse.

When he stopped in front of me, I acted as though I was a normal fare and jumped in the cab. The cabby asked me where I was headed and, as I took a quick a swig of my beer and then cleared my throat, I replied, "Southwest Philly" and gave him the address. It was at this point the games began.

I am certain this was not his first two o'clock rodeo, and he drew first blood by saying, "I'll tell you what, since it is late, let's do this run for a flat twenty dollars." Knowing I did not have a dime left to my name, I said, "Oh no, you can just run the meter", which was one clear indication that I was broke. Then he said in a more aggressive tone with an attitude, "How about fifteen dollars?" So I had to reply with, "No sir, I will pay you when we reach my house."

Instantly, he slammed the cab into PARK and my body lurched forward with the abrupt motion, almost spilling my beer. The level of his voice had modulated louder as he sneered, "You don't have any money, do you?" I replied, "No sir, not on me. It is at my house." The cabby was not in the mood for games so he pulled the cab off to the side of the road and told me to get the hell out!

For me to follow his directive would have meant I lost the game. I was not down for that since I felt he should not have passed by me the way he did. I went straight into my stereotyped college-prep-boy idiom voice and said, "Sir, whatever you do mean? All I did was flag you down so that I could get home. Please do not use that tone of voice and rude language with me. I have every intention to pay you. Trust me when I tell you I have more than enough money to pay for this ride, plus tip you. Please there is no need for the hostility or profanity." I lowered my voice just enough for him to hear me mumble, "I just do not understand people."

Game on. It worked…or did it? He peered in my eyes through his rearview mirror for a quick second, spun around in his seat, and then told me, "Okay, but you had better not be playing games." Then he put the cab into gear, pulled up to a sidewalk trashcan, and told me to throw away my beer. His voice was very demanding, so I followed his lead. He then pulled away, turned on the meter, and we headed to my destination in Southwest Philly.

He pushed his cab to speeds well above the limits for the streets of Philly, as if to see if I was going to produce his fare or else. Halfway there we came to a stop light and he spun around saying, "I want you to know that I am an ex-Philadelphia police officer" and I thought to myself, "So what! I am an ex-con."

Then the atmosphere in the cab went from hostile to life threatening. First, he told me that his cab was an old police vehicle. The suction sound of the automatic door locks confirmed that report. I had been in the back of enough cop cars to know he was on point. He wanted me to know he meant business and was going to win this game.

Next, he said, as he lifted up high enough so I could see his 'Big Bertha' .357 long…"If you are playing any games with me, I will blow your freaking head clean off your shoulders and will tell my cop friends that you tried to rob me!" Now he left me no choice, no wiggle room, and I had to win, although

I was cornered. The game I was playing with was my life, but I yelled to him anyway, "You can forget about getting a tip!" He responded, "Keep your damn tip, just have my money or else!"

The rest of the ride neither of us said a word. My mind was on point and I was planning my next move – running for my life. My plan was simple. I had given him a crack house address that was abandoned, so once I got in, I could run through the house and into the alley and make my getaway.

As we drove to the street with the crack house, my heart was pumping red Kool-Aid. I did my best to remain calm; never let them see you sweat, right? I told the cabby to pull over a few doors down, but he pulled right up to the address. I got out, told him I would be right back, and then casually walked up to the makeshift door that hid my get-away route.

That door would be my nemesis…it was propped up and held closed by a hinge that you had to lift up on in order to get in. If I were to get away from that crazy cabby, that door had better open like fluid running out a spout.

I tried once and the hinge would not move. I started to sweat and tried again. The hinge lifted, but now the door would not open; something was blocking it. I thought to myself, "I am done…That crazy cabby is going to shoot me dead where I stand!"

That was until I heard the familiar voice of a girl I often got high with, and just in the nick of time, too. I turned around to see that the cabby had stepped out of the car and was on his way over to investigate the situation. I had no room or time to play and I told the girl, in not such a nice voice, to 'open the damn door now!' When she did, I darted right past her and through the living room, dining room, through the kitchen, and out the back door.

Once outside, again my body had trouble keeping up with

my feet. I am not sure my feet even touched the sidewalk as I ran out the back of the crack house, jumping over the piled up trash. Thank God, I only had to go a half a block to reach the safety of a familiar house.

When I reached the yard, I leapt over the barbed wire fence, cutting my hands and legs wide open. I landed head first into the yard as I heard the cabby yelling into the alley, telling me to stop, and then he shot off his canon of a gun. That sound was all I needed to hear and gave me the energy to spring to my feet to continue my getaway.

It was the heat of the summer and the only thing standing between life and death was an air conditioner that was running full steam in the window. Without a second thought, I pushed the whole unit into the house and dove in behind it. Now I was faced with a gun behind me and a gun in front of me, pointed at my head by the old man who lived there, who thought it might be a home invasion.

I quickly announced myself and sealed the window tight, leaving the air conditioner running on the floor. It only took a hot second for them to realize I was in harm's way, especially after they heard the cabby fire off another three rounds into the darkness of the alley. On his way back through to his cab, he smashed anything he could get his hands on, including the young woman who saved my life by opening the front door of the crack house.

My safety net was once again Cheryl's daughter, who was upset with me as she attended to my cuts and told me to go upstairs and get some rest. Oddly enough, after all that, what I was most thankful for was that I was able to salvage my needed medication…the crack! *Are you serious?!*

I then decided to try my hand at what I did best, which was passing checks. I had a great deal of success running the game right in the heart of the city, hitting up restaurants, deli shops, Chinese markets and pizza shops. I could take a personal check, with absolutely no ID, and pass it off for a travelers check or Visa check that was issued from a bank.

For example, the personal check was typed out for two-hundred dollars, I would purchase all kinds of items from the store, and then receive the change. My favorite was the pizza shop and the larceny with them came in the form of a big order. I would place an order of two-hundred dollars worth of food, however, I would write the check out for six-hundred dollars, walking out with the change and a boatload of food.

Better still, if I had no money and no check, but wanted to eat, I would place a large to-go order. While I was waiting, I would ask for a soda and two slices of pizza or a sandwich – something that was prepared much quicker than the entire order. They would bring me the small order, I would begin to eat, and then tell the clerk that I had to get something from my car or make a phone call, grabbing the soda and the remainder of the pizza or sandwich and leaving…never to return! *Are you serious?!*

One day, I thought I would run my game at this small Asian corner store in Southwest Philly. When I walked into the store, I heard a distinctive bell ring. From the start, I could tell that the owner was very much on guard and this was not going to be an easy sell.

Word of a man fitting my description and passing bad checks had circulated the Asian Community, so I went deep into my bag of tricks. I began with being as polite as possible, speaking a well-educated dialogue and smiling a lot, as I methodically began to choose items from his shelves.

Once I saw that he bought into my game, I asked him if he could make me several sandwiches. He jumped into action, only to stop as fast as he started. Something triggered him, he went directly to his cash register, and he began to ring up everything. This forced my hand as to how was I going to pay. Without hesitation, I presented a check.

The transformation took place right in front of my eyes. He went from wanting to help me to letting me know with the tone of his voice that he was not happy with my form of payment. He barked, "We take no checks." His statement was very firm. I assured him that I still wanted him to continue to make the sandwiches and that I would be right back with my wife who had the cash, which was a lie, of course!

Then he made the mistake and turned his back. I was so desperate to leave his store with something that I pulled a package of Pampers diapers off the counter – I thought I could get ten dollars for them on the street. I sat the package on the floor and pushed them with my left leg towards the door.

When I thought I was in the clear, I made my exit. I turned the corner into the aisle that led to the door and all I could feel was the rush. As I opened the door, I heard those bells, and this time they were alerting the storeowner that I was on my way out. As I moved swiftly with the Pampers in my hand, my thoughts were about getting as far away as fast I as I could from the sound of those bells.

Not more than six steps into my getaway, my thoughts were interrupted by those jingling bells, only this time they were followed by the sound of the storeowner ordering me to halt, in English and his native tongue. This guy did not know Ronald L. James because the words Halt, Stop, Freeze or Don't Move meant GO! GO! GO! and GO!...and I took off as if I had wings on my feet!

So, let us talk physics for a moment. There are some things faster than the speed of sound - a storm is proof of that. There was a storm headed my way…and it was in the form of gunfire. This guy meant business, unleashing his frustration with the sound of every pop I heard.

I literally felt the compression of one of the bullets as it zipped past my left ear. I darted down the street and into an alley, trying to find some safety. I found a patch of bushes and ducked behind them, out of breath and, probably for the first time in my life, fearful of the situation I found myself in. My heart was racing; I knew I needed to get off the streets.

By this time, cops were racing up and down every side street, lights flashing and sirens blaring. I waited only a short time before moving and quickly escaped into a nearby crack house. Once inside, everyone wanted to know what all the commotion was about and when I told them, they wanted me out of the house so I would not bring the heat to them. I was not going anywhere until things calmed down. It was almost an hour before that happened, and I was thankful I was still breathing at the end of it. *Are you serious?!*

By bouncing all around the city, I ran into a host of people with the same larceny of the heart as mine. People were always out to see what they could get from me and, because I wanted to get high, I mainly dealt with people who had quick access to cash or drugs. More times than not, this put me face-to-face with the drug dealer or the 'wannabe' drug dealer. People were unable to classify me, other than a crack head. I was very hard to read and used this to my advantage when I needed to play someone, especially the wannabe drug dealers.

My game went like this: I would go into the sporting goods store and place the order for twenty pairs of Nike Air Jordan's for the summer basketball league. I would then go back with a corporate check from a sponsoring company, fictitious of course, and walk out with the sneakers. I would find a drug dealer in the Spanish section of North Philly who would take them all from me. They had their sneakers, I had my cash.

At this point, whoever bought from me knew I was capable of acquiring good merchandise, and I would encourage them to place orders with me for whatever they wanted. I could get baby clothes, building supplies, sporting gear, musical instruments, electronics…you named it and Ron James was on it. When I came through with their order, I would gain their trust.

As long as they treated me fair and with respect, I remained on the up and up with my criminal integrity. For some unknown reason, as soon as the drug dealer realized I also smoked coke, his or her views about me would change and they either talked crazy to me or tried to cheat me.

When it came to the game of drugs, there were so many ways to cheat a customer. In my eyes, once they crossed that line they became fair game and I would then spin them as fast and as far as they would try to spin me. I would ask them for something on the I.O.U., knowing I did not intend to pay them back, yet I would promise them anything that would entice their larceny…the new playpen for the newborn, the rental car from the airport, anything they wanted.

When they gave me what I wanted, they would not see me again until I really came up with that item or other items I could sell. No matter what my story was, my excuse was always the same – 'you know I just got out of jail.' Somehow, being in jail was considered a free pass, so I played that card whenever I could. However, the sad thing was I did get locked up a lot.

When I was on top of my game, I played countless numbers of drug dealers, one after another for untold thousands of dollars. Well, believe it or not, I was flat broke again! After cleaning up and getting some well-needed rest, I hit the streets again and found myself on the north side of West Philly when I ran into a friend.

She was a beautiful brown-skinned sister who, like me, loved to live on the edge. She reminded me of the young Gypsy. She took nothing from no one and, knowing she was daring, I invited her to go clocking with me. I knew a female always added to the special effects and validated the scam.

The two of us headed up to Cityline Avenue. It was late, around two o'clock in the morning, and that was always a good bet for traffic. After being out for a short period, we ran into some luck when our first two clocks produced about twenty dollars, our third attempt gained forty dollars, and then we stopped a young college girl who was attending St. Josephs University; she was more than willing to try to help us.

We told her our car had broken down and we needed money to get a tow. This young woman gave us money and her information so we could repay her. We thanked her and left. As soon as we got back to our safe house, we got high. It was early in the morning when I had an idea…why not tap the well while it was still full? Meaning, why not contact this young woman again while the getting was good? I did not share my thoughts with my friend, I just told her to come with me.

We made our way out the door to a pay phone and I gave the young woman a call. I could tell she just woke up. We chatted and I began to tell her we needed one-hundred fifty dollars more to get our car fixed. She was very happy to help, so she agreed to meet us. Upon meeting and giving us the money, she noticed my clothes had grease marks all over them, which was staged on purpose to make this whole encounter seem very real. She wished us well with our repairs and went on her way. However, I was not done.

I created a payroll check, filled it out for several hundred dollars, and then called the young woman back. I shared with her I wanted to come by her apartment and drop off her payment. When we got there, she was so happy to see us. I told her I had made arrangements with my boss to have him drop my payroll check off, so I asked her to deposit the payroll check into her account, subtract out what I owed her, and then to please give me the change, which was around four-hundred dollars.

She said she would run to the bank and told us to stay at her place, get cleaned up, and she would be right back. She gave my friend some clothes to change into and, while she took a quick shower, I washed up. As soon as I was done in the bathroom, I walked out right as the young woman was entering the apartment. She handed me the change and walked into her bedroom. This was the signal for my exit, so I walked right out her front door and kept moving, leaving my friend behind. *Are you serious?!*

On March 29, 1990, a year after my arrest in Springfield Township, I was booked in Philadelphia and handed over to lower Gwynedd Township Police Department. My paper-trail days of wheeling and dealing had come to a screeching halt.

<u>Philadelphia Police Department</u>: charged with forgery, bad checks and criminal attempt.

<u>Lower Gwynedd Township Police Department</u>: charged with criminal conspiracy theft by deception, 2 counts theft by deception, 3 counts receiving stolen property, 5 counts of forgery, criminal attempt theft by deception, criminal attempt

receiving stolen property, retail theft, criminal attempt forgery, criminal attempt bad checks, and 6 counts of bad checks.

Lansdale Police Department: charged with criminal conspiracy theft by deception, criminal conspiracy receiving stolen property, theft by deception, receiving stolen property, and 4 counts of forgery.

Montgomery Township Police Department: charged with 2 counts theft by deception, 4 counts of forgery, bad checks and receiving stolen property.

Lower Merion Township Police Department: charged with 4 counts, theft by deception, 2 counts of receiving stolen property, 4 counts of forgery and 3 counts of bad checks.

Yeadon Police Department: charged with theft by unlawful taking or disposition, theft by deception, receiving stolen property, forgery and bad checks.

Hatfield Township Police Department: charged with criminal conspiracy, theft by deception, receiving stolen property and forgery.

Media PSP: charged with theft by deception, receiving stolen property and bad checks.

Whitemarsh Township Police Department: charged with 4 counts of theft by deception, 4 counts of forgery and 4 counts of bad checks. Conshohocken Police Department: charged with 2 counts of theft by deception, 2 counts of criminal attempt theft by deception, criminal attempt forgery, forgery and bad checks.

Ten police departments in all. With all my violations and probation requirements, I was being bounced around like a ping-pong ball going to different court appearances. This kind of regimen, going in and out of prison each week, if not every day, was taking a toll on me.

I was not in jail a hot second before I realized a number of things. First, I knew I needed help and second, I wanted to go home. I knew I was in trouble and I quickly turned to God. I prayed for a few days and I felt very bad about a lot of things, one in particular was how I treated the young college student who was special and truly had a heart of gold. She did not deserve what I had done to her, and I felt compelled to call her and say something. I made a call to her.

When she answered, it took me a minute to get myself together, but I told her everything. She was not like the others I chose to hurt. She had no larceny in her heart. She did things for people out of her love for Christ and said her parents always encouraged her to reach out to those in need; her actions proved every bit of what she claimed.

After about five minutes of confession on my part, she said in a low defeated voice, "So the check you gave me was no good either?" I confirmed her fears by telling her the check was worthless. The phone went silent until she finally said, "May God bless you." I could tell tears were running down her cheeks.

If her tears had a voice, they would have been singing in perfect harmony with the tears that were streaming down my face. You would think this experience, and my reaction to it, would have made more of an impact on me and given rise to a change in me...you would think, right?!

Well, a few weeks had passed and I was moved from Intake to a pod in the new Montgomery County Correctional Facility in Eagleville, PA. I had lots of rest, three square meals every day, and I was feeling somewhat back to normal. I headed out to the pod to watch some television, which had on the evening news. I was sitting up front so I could hear what was going on in the world. Sometimes it is difficult to hear anything in jail with all the sounds of men yelling to each other, even though they were only two feet apart.

The big story for the day was that there had been a big robbery and a fatal shooting. News like that will get everyone's attention! A storeowner in West Philly protected the honor and safety of himself and his establishment by gunning down the would-be robber.

What first caught my attention was the fact that this shooting took place in Southwest Philly. I felt like a ton of bricks came crashing down on me and, as I looked closer at the television screen, I recognized the neighborhood, the store, the storeowner, and then I broke out into a cold sweat. It was the same Asian storeowner that shot at me several weeks earlier!

I stood there, my eyes glued to the tube, while my heart raced for understanding. My life literally flashed before me. The television cameras focused on the ground where the shell casings laid numbered. The area was taped off and they showed the ground where the victim was killed. The small voice that had always been with me spoke loudly, "That could have been you!"

All kinds of questions began to flood my mind and one kept repeating itself, "Why was I spared?" I realized at that very moment the only difference between the dead man and me was that each of those bullets that came my way were covered in mercy...even the one that should have taken my life.

CHOICE SIX
PRINCESS D

I RECEIVED A SENTENCE of two to seven years for my violations with the ten police departments. This time I would be heading up state and all I could think about were the stories I heard about life on the inside at the "Big House". I was shackled and cuffed, and the van ride was all about obeying every order shouted at you. Going up state for those at Montgomery County Correctional Facility was really just like traveling across town. SCI Graterford was a twenty-minute drive to a town called Collegeville, PA.

As we approached our destination, the first thing I noticed was the massive fifty-foot wall that surrounded the entire place. I was about to enter a whole new world, a world where the inmate was king. So there I sat with about forty other men in a small Intake cell and, like me, these men were brought here from other county jails from around the state. The first thing all of us had to do was strip down to our birthday suits and we were issued bright yellow-gold jumpsuits.

It had already been a long day. I had been awakened at four o'clock in the morning, rushed down to county lock up, placed in a holding cell, and there I sat for hours with the others who were going upstate. This process in and of itself should be enough for the average person to stop and think about what he or she had done to land them in jail.

You are crammed into a very cold room for five to six hours with other inmates going to court or other prisons, stripped searched, and yelled at to sit down, stand up, or whatever else the guards feel like commanding. You are shackled, cuffed and turned over to police detectives or sheriffs who command some more. You then go to your destination and when you return, it is the same kind of treatment. You are so tired that you cannot wait to get back to your cell.

In my case, I never considered prison home, but there I was, beat up, broken, with my ego bruised, and I was too proud to show any of that. I kept my 'mean man' mask on to keep others away and, trust me, I was not alone.

As I looked around the room, I was able to see all types of men wearing all types of masks. At first, the room started out in dead silence, which was typical for all holding cells with groups of men; no one wanted to break the ice. My guess was that no one wanted to say the wrong thing; however, in every crowd there are always two types that break the ice – the "know-it-all" guy and the "jokester".

In most cases, the-know-it-all goes first. He thinks he is tactful by opening a conversation with a question just to bait someone to give an answer that he already knows. The more he talks, the more everyone realizes that he is a liar. Somewhere along the line his story folds and he is exposed for what he really is. The only reason people opened up to him was for information, so he usually gains ground real fast, but when someone asks him a pointed question or challenges his credibility, he is drowned out by his own B.S. that cannot be trusted.

The jokester, on the other hand, makes light of everything.

The system, the guards, and even the people next to him are fair game. To him, everything is a joke and even though no one enjoys being the target, everyone wants to laugh. The jokester always hunts for the weakest inmate and exposes their fears, but usually because the jokester is actually the one scared to death and covering up his own fears.

None the less, the ice was broken and before I knew it, the room erupted into a windfall of conversation that covered every topic under the sun from women, sports and music... then back to women. That sort of chatter seemed to put everyone at ease and ninety percent of the masks the men were wearing were taken off.

Only the guards, who finally came to the door and called out ten names, broke the mood. Every inmate wanted to know what was going on. The guards left and locked the door, leaving us all in suspense. It was not until I was called that I found out what was going on.

I had to change into state-issued blues to go through the classification process. Everyone entering into the Pennsylvania State System had to go through this process. Once I was classified, I was re-issued state browns with a big D.O.C. (Department of Corrections) printed on the back...and I was now state property.

One by one the men from the holding cell were called for processing and before long, we were all together again and the room was alive with discussion. Only this time, the conversations were different. Everyone seemed to complain about this or that – their pants were too small, too long, their shirts were missing a button, their shoes came with no laces, and some men got brown boots while others got black shoes. No one seemed to be grateful, including me.

Not long after that we were fed cold lunches out of brown

bags – food was always a morale booster, but this particular meal was questionable. Once lunch was over, the process started up again and a number of men were called out for photos, finger printing, hearing tests and eye exams.

We also received an official state number, mine was BJ-2279. I was told from that point forward I would be called upon and referred to by this number, so I was to memorize it. During this process, we were asked a series of questions. I cannot recall all of them, but this was a true reality check not only for me, but also for everyone.

I was told to sit down in front of a state employee who was dressed in a tan uniform, unlike the guards who were dressed in gray and black. This person asked me all kinds of questions, which I recall being ready for. Having been questioned so many times previously by all kinds of police, marshals, detectives, and prison staff alike, I was used to the drill. Nothing really caught me off guard…that was until I was asked, "Where would you like your body sent in case you do not make it?"

The smile I wore on my face immediately ran for cover. As I was trying to process what exactly this person was saying to me, my mouth blurted out, "Excuse me?!" The question was repeated with clarity, "To what address would you like the state to mail your body in case someone kills you or you die while you are here at SCI Graterford?"

From that moment on, I realized my life had some value… if nothing more than shipping cost! The reality of the situation was becoming clear to me and this was not an amusement park or some sort of game. I know the things I practiced on the streets were not going to be tolerated in prison. I made up my mind right then and there to never get high or use drugs in prison…period. My focus was to get the hell out of that place in one piece! I never considered dying in prison and I was not going to entertain that thought at all, but I answered, "Send me to my mother's address."

It was a considerably long day and nearing eight o'clock at night when we were all escorted to see the doctor for health checks, and then escorted to Graterford's Open Bed Unit. We were assigned bunks in an area that held more than one-hundred fifty men. There was a shower area, four toilets, and absolutely no privacy. It was dirty, smelly and very loud. The atmosphere was ripe for just about anything. There was stealing, fighting, yelling and an 'anything goes' mentality that only the strong could and would survive.

You had the wolves and the lambs, but in my case, I was neither. Somehow, I was protected, able to run in the company of both the wolves and the lambs. I believe the prayers of my mother, grandmother and friend commanded God's love towards me. God responded once again by putting people in my life who cared about me and looked out for me…but still I ask why?

Just to give insight on cell life, nine out of ten of you will never get to choose your cellmate, and you will have to deal with whoever you are thrown into a cell with. It could be the first timer in for a DUI charge who is full of questions, right down to the no-nonsense, cut throat murderer. I have had them all.

One late night my cellmate and I got into a heated talk about something so simple that I do not even recall why we argued. This guy had been locked up for a violent crime, although his "claimed profession" was selling drugs. A native of Jamaica, he was living in upper New York and somehow got jammed in Pennsylvania. He stood five foot ten inches with a thin build and his disposition was mild mannered and very quiet. However, he was a killer and if you could stand to look him in the eyes, they could tell the story.

The argument escalated to the point we were cursing at each other. Then suddenly he shut down and had nothing else to say, almost as if he was calculating his next move. I sat down on the bottom bunk where I slept and he hopped up to the top. I later found out that in a small cell with bunk beds, the advantage always goes to the person who has the top bunk. Go figure!

I fell back and started thinking about our argument and it made me flaming mad, I mean mad to the point where my heart was racing. I thought about jumping out of my bunk, putting my boots on and snatching him off his bunk so we could mix it up. I had a better idea though – I decided to threaten him. I knew this would put him in his place and send a message of fear directly to his heart. I sat up in my bunk, and in my best North American grizzly voice, I told him, 'you had better not go to sleep tonight'.

My words rang off the small cell walls and I knew I made my point because everything remained silent as I lay back down to get some sleep. I felt victorious, excited from all the events that took place. It may have taken me about an hour to settle down and when I did, I started to realize whatever I was so mad about a few hours earlier really was no longer such a big deal. I just wanted to make amends and have peace back within the cell.

I started to drift off when I heard my cellmate clear his throat. I knew he was about to say something, maybe he was going to apologize…yes, that was what he was about to do. I thought to myself, "Good, and then I will do the same." He called out my name in his low Jamaican voice…I thought, "Okay, here it comes and I will finally get some sleep and things will go back to normal." He said, "Hey Ron, don't you go to sleep either."

WHAT THE HELL JUST HAPPENED? What happened to the anticipated apology? His words were not like mine…they did not bounce off the walls…no, his words pierced my soul. For the next six hours I just stared into the dark. I listened to his every move. I was gripped with fear, tormented by my own words. The law of reciprocity had its way and my words came back to agonize me.

The next morning I asked for his forgiveness. Yes, I humbled myself and apologized so we could move forward and, after a good laugh, things were back to normal. The two of us ended up becoming good friends, but I have heard stories of situation just like mine where the results ended up with someone dying.

Upstate prison life was worse than county prison, and the Federal penn life was an altogether different world – like Upstate on steroids! Fights, stabbings and drug wars were the norm from the eyes of the inmates. The guards and correctional officers even had their own rules of life in the Federal penn that involved random lock downs, recounts, drills and loss of privileges to the commissary, yard or even outside visitors.

They commanded you to stop, go, stand up or sit down whenever and wherever they wanted. They did not allow more than four people in a group, and broke up any conversation just because they could. If you saw them coming with an inmate in custody, you had to turn your back and not look their way. If they saw you looking, or even if they did not, they took your ID and you ended up in the hole for not following a direct order.

The point is that Federal is a no-win situation, and if you

argue, it only gets worse. It comes down to one-hundred percent control and one-hundred percent compliance, end of story. I personally had seen enough and was ready to get the HELL out of there. After meeting with the Probation and Parole Board, I was granted parole. I had done my 2 years and wore my Upstate label on my chest very well. But first, I had to go back to Bucks County Prison for a short period of time to satisfy their detainer. So finally, the day came when I was able to settle my bill with Bucks County and I packed up, said good-bye to prison and moved in with mom.

Mom was so glad to have me home. I played the role of the good son for only a short period of time before I ended up doing the same things I had done so many times previously. I know, you are probably shaking your head right now, not surprised at my actions. Believe me, the more I look back on this period of my life, I shake my head too! Yet, the times I was going through never made an impact enough to make me change.

My state parole officer was on my case from the start. He was nasty, I did not get along with him, and mom did not care for him either. Although, the problems I had were not with him, but rather me. I stopped reporting after the second visit and I went on the run. Back in those days, the parole board did not care much about a petty case like mine. If I would not have allowed police contact, they would have allowed my parole to expire, end or stop. But no, not Ronald James. I wanted to give the system a run for its money and it did not take long for me to get caught…again!

I believe I was out a total of sixty days before I was behind bars with new charges, a violation of parole, and sent back upstate. For some odd reason, the word recidivism is brought to the forefront of my mind. It is one of those words when

I first heard it I had no clue of its meaning. The dictionary defines the word as a tendency to relapse into a previous condition; especially relapse into criminal behavior. That was my lifestyle and it was the lifestyle of anyone who indulged in illicit drug use and/or alcohol addictions, which seemed to be everyone I hung around with. Now, I will provide some unknown, but striking facts about crime rate.

In the 1950's, the penitentiaries were few in number and were full of men who had committed horrifying crimes, such as first degree murder, rape and kidnappings. The stats revealed that the majority of these inmates were white males. I am not saying anything more than those who dominated the prison population during this time were whites.

By the 1960's, a change in the tide began to occur. I believe the reported gang violence that erupted in the major cities and the streets of Philadelphia may have contributed to what it has transitioned to today. These boys, young men and babies, were willing to defend their "corners" at all cost by fighting, stabbing and sometimes shootings to uphold their honor.

They were shipped off to youth study centers and reform schools, which were just mini-penitentiaries and prisons in disguise. The purpose was so that they could be reformed. A lot of the boys made it through and came out men, putting the "corners" behind them and putting their lives in order. However, the majority of them did not.

Those that did not make it graduated to prisons like Homesburgh, Western, Camp Hill and Graterford when they hit adulthood. By then, it was too late because they had adopted a new mindset.

The mindset of the prison code was very clear cut and simple – us versus them. Us being the cons, and them being the system, the white man, cops, turn keys, guards, and let us not forget Uncle Sam.

Once these boys, now "men", were released back into society, they looked healthy and solid from body-building, lots of rest, and eating like kings. These men were prime candidates for an army of waiting women, and hence, the 1970's babies were on the way.

In the 70's, many men fell victim to few choices – serve your country, serve your time or serve yourself. Those who chose to serve self usually fell victim to drugs and alcohol, mainly dope, and ended up committing crimes to support their habit. Those who sold it, however, strolled with pride and flaunted their cars, women and money…and still managed to escape getting caught.

Either way the men of the 60's were not there for a majority portion of time for the babies of the 70's, which meant the mothers had to raise these children alone. Some made it and some did not. This also meant there was a growing breed of crime, and new crimes needed new laws…and more new prisons.

Babies in the 70's, who had little or no father-figures around, found strength in role models who had nice things, and that meant they focused on neighborhood drug dealers, hustlers and those who "flashed cash". They followed these role models and eventually fell victim to the game, which meant they, like their fathers before them, ended up in prison. Like father, like son, repeating the problem, repeating the cycle, and leaving their children behind. These were the lucky ones…there are those that followed the model and sometimes were killed in the game.

When the 1980's rolled around, the game changed for the worse. The streets were flooded with drugs, and both the

Hispanics and Blacks were being used to market this poison called cocaine. Cocaine was once labeled a rich man's high because they were the only ones who could afford it. That soon changed, too. This drug was now readily available for as little as ten dollars.

Later, it was mass marketed as 'crack', which was available for as little as three dollars. During the 80's, crack was king and not only were men running around crazy smoking it, me being one of them, so were the mothers of those babies of the 70's, which begs an interesting question – who was raising the children now that they had no fathers or mothers? The answer was simple and it was grandmothers, family members, the streets...or worse, when they became wards of the system. I am not saying that the foster care and juvenile centers could not help because some did make it through the system; however, most did not.

During this time, the crimes the youth were committing were becoming more violent. Instead of fighting over the corners of the 60's, it was now in some places the colors of the 80's gangs. Gangs were the streets new role models. They saw the money to be made from drugs and violence, and they simply capitalized on the situation.

When the 1990's hit, the cities were big on shutting down drug corners, gangs and violence, and that forced the dealers out into the suburbs. This meant that mainstream American, and the mainly white communities, were not only being affected by drugs, per se, but the violence associated with it.

Crimes committed to get money to buy drugs were now in their backyard and in their homes, forcing a greater need for more prisons, drug rehabs and centers. They popped up everywhere, and it has become a multi-billion dollar industry.

The babies were now making babies at an alarming

rate. The media painted the picture that if the crack head or criminal does not kill you, the twelve, thirteen or fourteen year old child who carries a gun will. Fear played a significant factor. We have yet to see the product of the children from the years 2000 - 2010 who had no father, mother, neighbor, family member or friends to look up to or raise them. They had to rely on themselves to find their way out of the concrete jungle, oppressed by the system and exposed to media wars, school killings, suicide and much more on a regular basis.

They have been educated by video games that promoted killings, kidnappings, carjacking and sheer violence with no repercussions other than losing the game and starting over. The constant influx of guns and drugs that appeared on the streets was…and still is…a vicious cycle.

My thoughts are this: I believe it is a well-planned scheme designed to target the weak. Their young minds will be filled with meaningless things at a young age. There will be traps out there for those who are foolish enough to chase them, and they will fall prey.

William Cooper in his book titled, *Behold the Pale Horse*, called it 'cause and effect'. We do "this" so they will do "that". It is time to wake up people! Call me crazy if you want, but my opinion is that slavery is on the horizon. Yes, modern day slavery, and the prison system is a very big part of what is about to come down the pike.

They are building bigger prisons every year to handle the over-crowding. The prisoner is the product for a multi-billion dollar industry. I believe there will come a day when two classes will form. Those who have been labeled, marked or tagged as felons, and those who are not. Those who are not labeled will pay big bucks to control those who are. It will be this system that will dictate what we can do, buy and where we can go.

I said all that to say I have witnessed drugs and alcohol bring men, including me, back to jail no sooner than being released. Case in point: I ran into a close friend again, Willie, my boy who taught me everything about jail when I first got locked up. Willie was also back in because of a violation. The two of us celled up together and made a pact to commit crime better. *Are you serious?!*

How did we come up with this new plan? We spent every moment talking about getting more money by improving our crime skills. I found out this was a normal practice for repeat offenders. Many convicts or people doing time met up with like convicts to put their imaginations together - for the most part to improve on crime, set up contacts, or put new scams together. Prison was like an institution of higher learning and one day they may even award degrees with all the educating going on, just like college!

This particular day, Willie and I were outside working on our improvements. There were probably four-hundred plus men in between the block that day. It was a really nice day, even for being in prison. The sun was out, men were playing cards, chess or walking around and just enjoying the weather. There were no tables so almost everyone copped a spot on the grass.

We were midway down the yard going over our plans so that our next move would be our best move, and what we were going to do once we were out. I was facing the only door in the yard that led into the building. From a distance, I saw three brothers moving toward us with a purpose, marching in line just like soldiers. My boy and I continued to talk, but them getting closer and closer distracted me. I assumed they were

Fruit of Islam since the leader of the pack was bald-headed, clean-shaven and the clothing he wore was creased and tight. I also noticed he was carrying under his arm what appeared to be a folded up newspaper.

Then, without notice, the trio stopped about ten feet in front of us. I tapped Willie on his arm and pointed to them. He casually turned his head to see what I was talking about. He did this very smoothly as not to draw attention to whatever I wanted to show him. My eyes remained glued to the situation at hand. I was clueless to what was going on, but I could feel that something was not right…and I was right. As we kept talking, all I heard from Willie was blah, blah, blah, and he made no sense as I was concentrating on that trio.

Just then, I saw a ten-inch ice pick slide out from the confines of the newspaper. When the paper hit the ground, the ring leader marched towards his target of a group of white men sitting on the ground playing cards. He focused his sights on one man in particular, and when I saw who he was headed towards, I realized I knew the young man from my block. He was the go-to guy if you wanted tattoos and he was in trouble.

The ring leader rolled right up behind him and the young man never saw him. The first blow hit my soul as the ring leader stabbed him with that ten-inch ice pick right on the side of his neck. The two other men who were playing cards with him sprung to their feet and fled for safety in separate directions.

By this time, the young man was hit with several more blows to the back and the chest. To add insult to injury, all three men punched and kicked him.

I never heard Willie say, "Ron, let's go!", but he was already up on his feet and heading away from the scene. I only realized this because he literally had to come back for me. He grabbed my collar and pulled me forcefully and then I understood it was time to make an exit.

As we left the scene, I overheard the ring leader telling the wounded tattoo artist the reason behind why he was attacked. All I heard was, "Don't you ever go near my lady again!" From a distance, I saw the ring leader drive the ice pick into the ground with a rock so no one could ever locate it.

By this time, a crowed had formed and somehow this almost dead young man made it to his feet and staggered through the crowd towards the front door. His friend that had abandoned him earlier now took a rock and broke the window to the main hallway. This alerted the guards and once they came and saw there was someone injured, they got him on a medical cart.

The yard was immediately put on lockdown for an investigation. About fifteen minutes later, we heard a Medi-Vac helicopter come to transport the young man because of his serious injuries. He could have died; however, I received word weeks later that he pulled through.

I realized that life was truly not a game, especially in prison. So what was wrong with me that I kept subjecting myself to this type of lifestyle? I was trapped by it, but I loved it; it was a vicious cycle.

My boy Willie was paroled first, then it was my turn...or so I thought. Before I could hit the streets, I found out I had a charge from my past that had come back to haunt me.

<u>Upper Merion Township Police Department</u>: charged with theft by deception, receiving stolen property, 3 counts of forgery and bad checks from 1989. I pleaded guilty to a 2-year sentence that ran this current charge with my already imposed sentence. In my eyes, I thought I had caught a break, but the reality of the plea would one day show its ugly face.

So finally, it was my turn and I was paroled back into society again. I went home to live with my mother and, as soon as I crossed her threshold, I gave her a big kiss, got on the phone, and called Willie. We met up and quickly put our plan into action. I wanted him to see just how sweet the paper game was.

I will spare you the details, but when you do the same things – checks, drugs, alcohol and women – you get the same results. So there I was once again sitting at a police booking desk! When the officer asked me my name, I gave them an alias name and a bona fide license, not of myself, of course!

They were looking for someone else – someone who had been trying to pass checks at a jewelry store. Well, it just happened to be one of the ID's that was in my coat pocket, but I was not going to let on to that fact. My game was no match for these officers; I knew the drill all too well. However, I forgot they had the option of searching me, and after they completed a thorough one of my person and the U-Haul truck we were using, they came up with what they were looking for and then some.

They found four sets of ID's and I was up the creek without a paddle. On the other hand, my partner Willie had no ID on him and gave them an alias. After being booked, we went to court and bail was set at five-thousand dollars cash for me and two-thousand dollars cash with ten percent to post for him; he walked.

On March 8, 1994, <u>The West Whiteland Township Police Department</u>: charged with 2 separate cases of receiving stolen property, criminal conspiracy, theft by deception, forgery bad check, false reports to law enforcement, theft by unlawful taking to dispose and unauthorized use of auto and vehicles.

Tredyffrin Township Police Department: charged with forgery, theft by deception, receiving stolen property, false reports to law enforcement, unsworn falsification to authorities, bad checks, unauthorized use of auto and vehicles.

I was transferred from the West Whiteland Police Department to Chester County Prison, called Chester Farms. I had been processed under the alias name I had given them and never corrected it, hoping that I would make bail before anyone realized. It did not take Willie long to come up with the money, but it was too late and they had realized their mistake. Therefore, I then had to go to court on my new charges, under my real name, and it was clear that I would be going back upstate to serve time for those charges after serving time in county prison for all the other charges.

I quickly got a job on the county prison's paint crew, and then I moved to the maintenance and woodshop department. My hard work brought me favor with the staff and the warden. When it was time to go back Upstate, I asked those in charge if I could do my state time at the county and, to my relief, the request was granted by the warden.

He told me that he was pleased with the reports he heard about me, as well as my hard work. God's timing could not have been any better. I say this because the warden was about to retire and the incoming warden would not have been as gracious.

It was at Chester County Farms that I met Princess D…and the reason for this chapter. My mom had nicknamed her and she was an inmate in the female section of the prison. Since I worked on the maintenance crew, I was able to move around the prison, and it was in the women's section that I had the honor of meeting her.

This five foot, seven inch white princess had ocean

blue eyes that pierced to the depths of my heart and I was literally blinded by love. This full-figured, full-busted female overflowed with charisma and persuasiveness, using whatever it took to con, exploit, control, manipulate, influence and lie to have her way...I LOVED IT!

When it came to selfishness, I had met my equal! This girl had more game than Parker Brothers, yet I could not get enough of her. So much so that I married her – yes, you read that correctly. I married Princess D while I was still married to Cheryl.

Okay you got me. I was guilty of polygamy, too, but I could not help myself! The marriage between us took place well before either one of us said "I Do". After first meeting her on the women's block, we began to write and slip notes to each other. The two of us had jailhouse experience; however, she was craftier then I was, and this was by no means her first stay at Chester County Farms.

Not only was she writing me, she was also writing several other men and when I confronted her about the situation, she lied, stating, "They were just friends". I wanted to believe her, but Princess D was out for Princess D...and who was I to cast the first stone? I had been hitting on a nurse who worked in medical, so my own selfish acts were also in full progress.

It was about this time that I became deathly ill. One day I went back to the block because I felt a little light-headed. My heart started to race as I sat on my bunk. It slowed down as quickly as it started, so I thought nothing of it. I grabbed my mug of ice cold water, took a sip, and then sat back to rest some more.

Within seconds, my heart began to race again, only this time in abnormal, crazy beats. I stood up, called my cellie over, and told him what was going on - that I thought something was very wrong. He looked at me and saw that I was serious.

I grabbed his hand and placed his palm on my chest. His reaction more than likely saved my life. He snatched his hand back like I had placed it on a hot stove. He told me, "Yo! You need to get up to medical now!", and if his facial expression was any indication of what he was witnessing, I was sold. His eyes went straight to fear.

My only problem was that it was time for lock up and count would be soon. I moved as fast as my feet would carry me towards the upstairs gate leading to the main hallway. The guard at the gate that night had a lot of respect for me, so when I said I needed to get to medical, he never questioned what I was trying to do. All I said to him was that something wrong with my heart and I had to get to medical. He pushed the buttons and I was buzzed through.

You have to understand that this was God in full action. Out of all the prisons I had been in, the prisoner did not get to call the shots. If there was a medical emergency, issue or problem, the guards, C.O.'s or staff would tell you to fill out a request slip and get in line. If by chance it was an actual emergency, they would call for a code. God's mercy was in action all right, and I was able to make it to the hallway that led to medical. I was out of breath and soaking wet from perspiration, but I had made it.

By now, my mind was in complete sync with my heart - they were both running crazy, I was totally disorientated and needed help. I spotted Amanda and Gi-Gi, two very friendly nurses who also respected me and whom I now consider angels from above. They were sitting outside of medical on a bench taking a smoke break and I called out to Amanda as

I staggered towards her. All I had the energy to say was "My heart, something is wrong with my heart".

I was keyed into medical, but both nurses still did not understand the seriousness of the situation; they were in a playful mood. It was only after Amanda saw my condition that the fun and games went out the window. She quickly went into her nursing bag; it was time to go to work. She grabbed her blood pressure cuff, wrapped it around my arm, and then stuck a thermometer into my mouth.

The panic began when she tried to get a read on my vitals and my blood pressure was off the chart. She started to shake; I knew at this point I was in bad shape. She called Gi-Gi over for assistance, asking her to see if something was wrong with her cuff, and to get a second read on the blood pressure. These two nurses started to dance and move in sync all over the medical department.

Amanda grabbed a pen and wrote my blood pressure directly on my arm. She then noticed my temperature was sky high, so she immediately picked up the phone and called for outside medical back-up. They brought me an oxygen tank and placed a mask over my mouth and nose because I was having trouble breathing. All I knew at this point in my life was that I did not want to die and I certainly wanted to live, but I knew that I was in bad shape.

When the paramedics arrived, they took control and immediately hooked me up to an I.V. Their goal was to somehow break the sporadic rhythm of my heart. They quickly gave me a dose of adrenaline by forcing it into my bloodstream, but nothing happened. They tried something like morphine, but my heart was still beating crazy. Something was definitely wrong and I felt my life was slowly coming to an end.

I started to drift in and out of consciousness. I recall asking God to help me. As I looked up, I noticed Amanda never left my side. Once again, God had placed a host of angels all around me, and my girls Amanda and Gi-Gi were among them.

The medics were on the phone with the hospital, and next thing I knew, I was strapped down and transported to West Chester Hospital. After I received multiple series of tests and asked many questions by every medical person that entered my room, it was finally determined that I had Graves' disease, which was a hyperactive thyroid.

I had to wonder about the cost the county incurred for that five-day hospital stay, with all the tests and correctional officers babysitting me around the clock, but that was one of the advantages of being a prisoner!...if you consider that to be an advantage!

When the doctors determined the condition was under control, I was returned to Chester County Farms and everyone, including my boss, the nurses, guards, staff, inmates and Princess D were happy to see me. I was told to take it easy and that meant I was able to move around the prison, but I was not required to do much of anything.

It seemed as though my illness gave me favor with the administration and eventually I was able to get a job over at the prison's pre-release center...and guess who else was there? Princess D! It was there I had the chance to talk to her every day, and it was only a matter of time before we became an item. It was not long after that when we both were released and it was game on!

I bet it did not take two weeks before I had a U-Haul truck and moved her things into my mom's house with me. Princess D and I had become very close, and she and my mom became girlfriends. They enjoyed each other's company and spent hours talking about life, while I set up myself to do 'me' things.

I started out okay - I had found work, reported to my parole officer as required, stayed clean, and I had Princess D as a girlfriend. Unfortunately, the selfishness always seemed to surface and when it did, things ended up getting ugly, out of hand, and out of control. I went right back to wanting to get high, and this time I took Princess D with me. She seemed to maintain her control, but I had none and was totally out of control. It was as if each time I got high and went to jail, the craziness stopped, but as soon as I was out of prison and picked up where I left off, my life got crazy again…and this time was no different.

My lifestyle was no match for normal living and it began to put unwanted pressure on my mom. To make matters worse, I had started to steal from the house and I ended up taking her only television. I had stolen from the one person who never turned her back on me, so that should give you an idea of what I would do to someone I did not know.

Princess D was outraged with my behavior and demanded that I replace my mom's television and get myself together. She cared about me, but she could not stand to see my mom in pain either. After replacing mom's television with a brand new one, it was time for us to move out, and rightfully so, plus my parole officer was now hot on my trail for failure to report.

Princess D and I hit any hotel, motel, Holiday Inn we could find, and life was anything but normal. I enjoyed living on the edge, but something about living on the run and getting high just set me off. I was delusional, paranoid, scared and never could find peace.

Each time we checked into a place, I would barricade the hotel doors with furniture, place a wet towel at the base of the door to prevent someone from smelling or detecting the drug's odor, and made sure that windows were closed and the curtains shut. If there was a peephole, I stuffed paper in it. I turned the radio or the television volume up to cover any sounds we made and unplugged the phone. I literally created my own prison cell. I did not want anyone to know we were there, and I certainly did not want them to find out we were getting high inside.

This meant anyone and everyone – management, the stickup boys, the police, or anyone I robbed, scammed or stole from. The lifestyle was horrific and I hated it, but I could not break away from it. Keeping the outside world away seemed easy in comparison to what I was experiencing inside the room. The problem was me, the problem was Maggie Mae, and now the demons I began to see became a problem, too. When I got high, I was able to enter another world... remember, I told you things got worse.

No sooner would I strike a match to burn some crack than an army of demonic forces would arrive to assault every aspect of my being. Everything I had set up to protect, Princess D and I tore down. I literally took on these forces in the flesh, while they toyed with me in the spirit. I yelled at them and cursed them out with all my might.

I was a mad man, and there were times when I chased them into the hotel's hallway, standing there butt naked with a glass crack stem in my hand. There were times when I tore up rooms in search of answers. I looked in toilets, cut open mattresses, searched drawers, behind mirrors and pictures on the walls. I pulled up carpets, unscrewed electric outlets, took apart fire alarms – nothing went untouched.

When I was done, the room usually looked like an Iraqi war zone and there I stood, sweating, out of breath, and smack in the middle of my own mess without a clue as to why. What took place was real to me, but to someone on the outside, I was a crazed lunatic. I was certain the answer was in any one of those hotel rooms. I just never thought to search in that book that the Gideon's left behind.

After I came down from the high, it would finally hit me and I realized that I needed to protect Princess D and our freedom so, once again, I would take the time to put things in order for our safety. I would hide the crack and everything else that could send us back to jail.

Do not think for one minute that Ron James was crazy! No, I was very much in my right mind. I always found something in my searches, and that was enough to keep me going. I found cash, other people's drugs, crack pipes, stems and all kinds of other fun things.

You may ask where Princess D was when I was doing all of this? She was a trooper by nature and she was with me because she wanted to be, and it was that way until the end. She remained by my side through all that craziness. Maybe she was crazy for staying with me. Nonetheless, she protected me and understood me.

When I had made a mess, she helped me clean it up. If I had run out of the room, she was the one who pulled me back in. When I had started to dial strange phone numbers on the hotel's phone, she pulled the plug. Her main concerns were that we slowed down on doing drugs and that we always made sure to eat something. Best of all for me, at the end of the day, she was still there.

After hitting every known crack head hotel in the city, we grew weary, but could not give up the lifestyle. Princess D pleaded and begged me not to allow her to get busted in Philly – that was her only request. She had heard so many horrible stories about how the women were treated in the Philadelphia System, both by guards and inmates alike, and she wanted no parts of it.

I had often left Princess D behind in the room while I set out on my missions, but things were different after her request. I wanted to fulfill my promise to her and get us out of Philly. I took a payroll check and made a move to a sporting goods store that was still under the Telecheck System. I was able to walk out with two-thousand dollars worth of gear… for our fictitious company's fund raiser, of course!

After selling a few items for some needed cash, I was able to provide Princess D and myself with several outfits from head to toe, plus I stopped and bought us something to eat. It was one of the few times Maggie Mae was put on hold, but not for long…just long enough for us to rest and collect our thoughts.

I had no idea where we were going; we were moving wherever the wind blew us. The next morning we loaded up and we were off, heading across the bridge into New Jersey. I thought it would be a good thing to stop and get some beer and some directions to the nearest crack dealer. It did not take but a hot second to find what we were looking for…in Camden, and the cycle began to repeat itself. Was I crazy…? Do not answer that!

I knew Camden was a death trap, especially since I was chasing coke with a white girl on Hooke Alley and in the hotels across from the racetrack. Interracial relationships did not sit well in Camden, and I was putting both of us at risk.

After finding what we were looking for, we checked into a room that had to be the size of a prison cell – just the way I liked it. I went through my drill of fortifying us in the room, and I noticed there was not any kind of security on the door. No dead bolt, no chains, no latch, and no peepholes. Of course, that particular room did not need a peephole because the police or would-be robbers had kicked it in a few times and it sat ajar to the point where I could see clearly out into the parking lot. The space was about an eight inch gap, but it might as well have been standing wide open.

That small, soft voice I often heard was speaking to me again, only this time it was not so soft. I heard it loud and clear saying, "GET OUT!" Not just out of the room, but out of Camden, so our stay was short-lived and we headed north on I-95 to the next destination site.

Throughout the drive, we smoked crack and drank beer until we ran out of both, forcing us to stop in a city that was just as dangerous as the one we had left. We were now in Newark, New Jersey. We had an unfortunate event take place where we had spent forty dollars on some would-be crack from a would-be dealer, but the stuff ended up being crushed dry wall or chalk. So, we racked this one up as a loss, found a decent hotel in Clifton, New Jersey, and passed out from exhaustion.

The following day we hit a few stores and picked up some electronics. I did not have a good feeling about New Jersey, so we drove back to Philadelphia, unloaded our goods, and then hit the turnpike and headed west.

Our motto was, "to pass checks at any store that would accept our offer". I had a small suitcase full of checks, ID's and equipment to make more ID's if needed so this was going to be a long run. The suitcase was our lifeline and, ironically, we called it our 'bible'. We safeguarded it and made sure we kept it close at all times.

Our four-door Oldsmobile Cutlass had seen better days. It truly was on its last leg, but that did not stop us. As long as the car kept running, so did we. We made stops at various retailers and picked up some large lobster tails, a few cases of beer and cartons of cigarettes. However, the smoke from the car was now too obvious to ignore and, to make things worse, the car had started making odd noises, so we pulled off the highway in Harrisburg, PA. It was there that another event changed the course of our lives.

Our first stop was at a Pep Boys. We knew they took checks and figured on good service there. We were hoping a mechanic would at least look at the car and suggest what we needed to purchase. We were told they were not taking any more cars for the day and that we should return the next day. Normally that would have been acceptable if we had arrived late in the day, but it was still early with a lot of time left on the work clock. We pleaded with the manager to have someone look at the car, but again we were told no. We were not getting good vibes from anyone there, so we drove on looking for another place that would be more helpful. Not far from the Pep Boys, we saw an NTW shop and stopped. We were able to speak with the manager, and unlike Pep Boys, it was as if God's hand of mercy was in charge of that shop.

The manager opened the garage doors for us and told us to pull in. He put his technician to work on our car, and it was as if someone spoke to the rest of the team in the shop and they all came over and started to help.

The car could be rescued, but the state inspection was about to run out, the rocker arm was broken, the windshield was cracked, it needed a tune-up, new wiper blades, four new tires, a rear bumper and a dent in the rear side panel needed fixed. The only problem we ran into was that it would take a few days because the manager needed to call around for parts. He suggested a nice hotel that had a swimming pool and restaurant. He called a cab that drove us to the Days Inn and we actually spent time relaxing.

NTW called us two days later and said the good news was that the car was ready. The bad news was that the bill for all the labor and repairs was in the neighborhood of two-thousand dollars. On our way to pick up our car, Princess D questioned me as to how we were going to pay for it. I smiled and told her I had it all under control; however, the reality of the situation was that I was clueless as to how I would pay. I concluded I would have to call on my gift of check writing in order for us to retrieve our ride.

As soon as we got to NTW, I took control by allowing them to believe they were in control. I acted as if I needed the manager to run through every detail, explain what they had done to our vehicle, and justify their bill.

When the manager asked for payment, I asked Princess D to pass me the corporate check. I filled it out as if this was what I did all day long, which unfortunately it was. The manager said, "No problem, let me just run your check through our checking system." CHECKING SYSTEM?! My heart stopped and my mind raced!

I had already scanned the shop, but did not see any indication of a check system. I inquired with the manager as to what system they used and he responded with "Telecheck." This ride was about to crash! I had burned Telecheck out a long time ago with the ID I was currently using, but I held my composure; I refused to break! Simultaneously my mind was working on a plans B through Z.

The manager pulled out the little machine from under the counter and punched in the check's information and my phony driver's license number. In less than a minute, he received an approval number. There stood three people in complete shock! Princess D and I looked at each other and said OKAY...the manager smiled and told us that was the fastest approval he had ever witnessed. His response was, "Boy you must have good credit." We played right along, but the good credit that we had was far greater than we ever realized.

Today, I believe that credit was from God who showed his grace and mercy on us, and that credit had nothing to do with the car or checks and everything to do with the direction we needed to follow. Princess D and I were so happy that we began to give the manager and his workers all types of gifts. They appreciated everything, especially the case of beer.

Now that our car was running smooth, it was time to celebrate. We drove into the heart of Harrisburg and purchased some crack and then we headed back to the hotel. When we pulled up, I was feeling very cocky and told Princess D to drop me off at the office and that I would meet her back at the room. She never questioned my actions. She knew Ron James was up to something.

I waltzed into the office and requested to pay for the next day in advance. The hotel manager was happy to accommodate me. I pulled out my form of payment – a payroll check – made out to my alias in the amount of $600. He took the check, looked it over and asked me to endorse it. Then he walked over to the safe and cashed my check, handing me the difference. With the room paid for and cash in my pocket, I thanked him as I walked out of the lobby. When I got back to the room, I told Princess D what I had done and we spent the night smoking crack.

We realized the next morning that it was time to leave Harrisburg and continue on our journey. By the time we reached Pittsburgh, we were out of crack and needed to find the nearest dealer. About two o'clock in the morning we drove around downtown Pittsburgh looking for anyone who could help us with directions to the nearest drug dealer. The pickings were slim; however, I did find one guy who said we could find just what we were looking for in the St. Clair Village Projects.

Into the hills we went, leaving the beautiful Pittsburgh skyline behind. I recall fleeting thoughts of guilt and shame because I really wanted to treat Princess D to a special night downtown. What in the world was wrong with me? I hated the road I was traveling down, yet I was stuck in a rut and could not get out.

I knew all my life something was special about me and somehow my thoughts would lead me back to the path I was on as a child. I recalled the sidewalk that contained the cracks and how, as I walked further down the sidewalk, it became more broken, but then eventually went back to the smooth surface. I believe the event had something to do with the road I was now on and I refused to let go of the hope that things would turn out for the best.

My thoughts of me were interrupted when we saw the first signs of crack…and not the sidewalk kind either! We saw this young girl walking alone, along the side of the road with her hooker swagger in full swing, so we stopped to ask her for directions. All true crack heads will never miss out on an opportunity to get high and she was not about to let us go. She assured us that she knew where the best crack in the city was and that she could take us there. She started going into the crack head investigation mode, asking us twenty questions. I was not up for a lot of game or questions; I just wanted to get high. I assured her that we were not undercover cops by pulling out our caramel residue stems, which was a clear indication of fellowship.

The only problem we had was trying to fit her into our car. Our back seat was jammed packed with electronics, equipment and a variety of store bought items. There was literally no place for her to sit, but somehow she managed to squeeze in.

Our destination was down a long, dark street and Princess D and I looked at each other to make sure we were on alert. This girl was excited…too excited for me. She wanted to know how much we were going to spend and I pulled out the wad of cash, only to realize the mistake I had just made. In doing so, I spotted the girl's eyes glued on my cash so I passed it over to Princess D.

To make matters worse, after telling her I wanted to spend one-hundred dollars, she said she needed for me to give her the cash and she would be right back…yeah, right! I told her never mind and get the hell out my car. She then changed her tune and told me to follow her.

When we arrived at the spot, she begged me to just give her the money because she said the boys who sold the crack had told her never to bring anyone to their place. I stood my ground, but when one of the guys came out and yelled at her, I knew this was legit. I gave her the money and she disappeared into the house.

A few minutes later, I saw her coming and she moved with a purpose. She gave me the goods; however, she went back inside, which was very unusual since she had been so ready for a hit. This was odd to me, but I thought she was going back to get her cut from them so I continued to the car. Once inside, I tore into the bag and made sure it was good crack. The next instant, that girl came running and yelled to me to wait. She wanted her cut and I at least wanted to treat her fairly, so I dug into the bag and broke off a piece of rock for that girl and as I passed it back to her, I asked her to get out.

My thoughts were to get away from her ASAP! I just did not feel right about her, but she begged us to allow her to take one blast while she was in the car. I looked at Princess D, who gave me the nod of approval and went ahead with lighting up, but I was too upset to join in. My mind was still on this girl's strange actions and still was curious as to why she went back into that house.

The girl blasted and then started to dig around in her pockets, in her purse and into our things, and I had enough. I jumped out of the car, walked around to the back passenger's side, opened the door, and escorted her out into the street… and not a moment too soon. As I looked back down the street, out of the shadows, three guys were exiting the house and heading our way.

Without question, I knew what was in store. I jumped back into the car and sped off, getting clear out of Pittsburgh that night. We drove all around the outskirts looking for a hotel; however, there was some race in town that week and nothing was available. We were forced to keep it moving…once again God's grace.

Smoking our way to Columbus, Ohio, we found more crack there…enough to smoke our way into the state of Indiana. The crack stem was empty again, but we were tired and decided to pull off the highway and check into a hotel. The rest was definitely needed and when I woke up, I had no idea what time it was, what day it was, or where I was. I had no idea of current events, but I knew for sure that Princess D was safe and I was hungry!

I decided not to wake her since she had the real job of

looking after me while I did crazy stuff on crack, and she was due the rest. Therefore, I stuffed my pocket with cash and hit the streets to surprise her with breakfast. I had no intentions on getting high; I only wanted to do something nice for Princess D.

As I drove down the main highway, the first thing I spotted was not a McDonalds, Burger King or Wendy's. I spotted a sister that was very well put together from head to toe, and looked very much out of place that early in the day. I knew if I asked her anything, I would find my answer.

I pulled right up next to her and asked her to get in and, of course, she did. My next question was not about food or sex…I wanted to know who had the crack. Yes, okay, so much for not wanting to get high and doing something nice. I just knew this girl had to know where the crack was. She told me to continue driving straight ahead about two more blocks. If I would have kept driving on my own, I would have found crack alley for myself.

She wanted to know what I wanted to get and how much I wanted to spend. I told her one-hundred dollars and that made her tell me to keep driving because she wanted to take me to a dealer's home. That girl was sophisticated, not the typical crack head female or hoe on the stroll. No, she was polished and very much in control.

After a series of turns, I pulled over in front of a house and I handed her the one-hundred dollars. No fuss, no questions… one-hundred percent trust. I sat back in my seat and drifted off; I must have been more tired then I realized. When I came to, I know that at least thirty minutes had gone by. I looked all around for that girl, but she left nothing behind except a memory.

I truly had absolutely no clue which house she went in,

and I could not very well go knocking on any of the doors in this neighborhood. What was I going to ask? "Have you seen a pretty black woman who is supposed to be buying crack for me?" Ok, I admit it was a very bad choice giving her my one-hundred dollars not knowing who she was, where she was, or where I was for that matter.

I was about to call it a day, just find breakfast and return to Princess D. There was part of me that always cherished hope, and this experience was no different, so I waited another thirty minutes until I finally decided to admit that I had been burned. As soon as I turned the key in the ignition, I was startled by the sound of the passenger door opening, and there she stood.

She apologized and explained that her dealer friend had to break things down and put something together for her. I was handed the crack without a moment's hesitation...I liked her style. We pulled away and I drove to a side street off from the main stream of traffic. I was excited to give this product a try and, when I opened the package, I found it to be twice as much as I expected.

I reached in and handed her a nice portion and she said it was too much – more pointers in her favor. I took a blast and then gave her a mouth-to-mouth shotgun; her lips were soft and moist. Our eyes connected and I was in trouble! If I did not think long and hard about my next couple of choices, everything I knew of life at that moment would change. I sat back in my seat and thought long and hard.

I started the engine and she wanted to know if something was wrong. I smiled at her and gave her the assurance that whatever was going on had nothing to do with her. She asked me if I would mind picking up her daughter and I agreed. She then invited me back to her place and I wrestled with that thought, but something deep inside me told me no, and I fought off the pleasant temptation.

I thanked her for the offer and declined, stating that I needed to complete my mission. I had asked her and her daughter if they were hungry, so we stopped at a local McDonalds drive-thru and I purchased something for all of us, including Princess D, which was my original purpose. I knew if I went on the run with that beautiful woman, Princess D would wake up to nothing, and she trusted me enough to know I would always return.

When I walked through the hotel room door to our room, Princess D was awake and still in the bed. She was concerned about where I had been, but happy to see both me and the food.

A day later, I was out the door and headed for more crack of course. I was able to find some on my own, but it was nothing like what I had gotten from that young woman the previous day. It sustained us until the next search, and the next, and we did not stop when the cash was gone.

We then sold things out of the car for more drugs, and when those things were gone, we began to take orders from drug dealers for more retail items. We realized time was running out on this town and drugs had a way of bringing unwanted guests, so before that took place, we made one last hit on a sporting goods store for twelve-hundred dollars in gear, and then we packed up and headed out of state.

We had stopped at a rest area and I called my cousin Peanut, who was always someone I could count on and trusted. As always, the invitation was open for us to come his way, that had us excited and we found a new burst of energy.

When we arrived in Wichita, Kansas, we checked into a hotel and we all went out on the town. We partied at a local bar and ate like kings. From the very start, I dropped paper like it was going out of style, and with cash coming in fast, I turned it around to buy coke just as fast.

We checked into one of Wichita's finest hotels, bringing our own amenities of alcohol, weed and crack. The only time I really came to the surface was to purchase more crack.

A series of events were about to unfold that led us into holy matrimony. Princess D had been ready to land and I realized with the amounts of money we had pulled in and wasted on hotels, we could have purchased a really nice condo. We thought this would be the perfect opportunity to start fresh, so we headed to Oklahoma to visit a friend. It was our intention to get an apartment and settle down together. I asked a friend in Tulsa if we could shake it up with him until we could get our own place. That was the plan since I felt he owed me at least that from all my past dealings with him.

We began our drive to Tulsa with high hopes and somewhat clear minds, but the skies were about to unleash one of the worst rainstorms I ever recall witnessing. It was sunny out with not a cloud in the sky, feeling like the calm before the storm, and both of us sat silent and deep in thought for what this trip would bring. I looked over at Princess D from time to time. She was beautiful as she sat there and I felt so lucky to have her in my life.

The small voice inside my head kept telling me I needed to straighten my life out if I wanted to keep her, but my selfish attitude kept pushing those words down deeper inside of me. Princess D was the first to break the silence. She turned toward me as if she received some sort of sign or divine intervention and posed a question that brought me back to reality, "We have tried everything else, do you think we should try God?"

Her question was extremely well put considering I had

just dismissed that small voice in my head. I said nothing at first, but her look required an answer so I blurted out an unconscious 'yes' when deep inside I was struggling on how to commit to that answer when I needed to be sinfully selfish.

It was not long after that we ran into inclement weather... and I am not just talking a little 'ole rain cloud. It was as if the heavens opened and just drenched us with buckets of rain. The water on the highway was splashing up over our car, and even with the new wiper blades on high, the water would not push off the windshield. It was like driving under a constant waterfall.

As tractor-trailers passed, they sprayed so much water that the car would shake, there was zero visibility, the road disappeared, and all I could do was slow the car down until the truck passed. Inside the car, the two of us were shaking so badly from fear; Princess D was petrified. She wanted me to pull over and stop, but I was afraid someone would plow into the back of us because the lines on the road to tell which lane you were supposed to be in could not be seen.

The skies were so black and the only visible light came from the lightning that tore up the sky. Princess D began to weep; I pulled her close to me and she buried her head on my lap. The best I could do to comfort her was to rub her with my elbow while keeping both hands locked on the steering wheel, my eyes glued to the faintly visible truck taillights ahead of me.

I maintained a steady, slow speed and asked God to please pull us through. The rains lasted for about thirty minutes and then, as if nothing had ever happened, it stopped. We rested for the night and the following day we finished our trip to Tulsa.

We enjoyed our time in the car together and instead of

getting high, we talked, laughed, and had fun. We covered every topic under the sun, including marriage. I asked her if the door opened, would she be my wife and she smiled and said, "Sure." The seed was planted, so the only thing stopping me from popping the question was me.

When we hit Tulsa, we were eager to locate my friend. I got him on the phone and he guided us to his apartment. We were invited in and made to feel right at home. I knew this was just the start we needed. After a few beers and a meal, my friend mentioned his roommate, which he had not done before, and suddenly a bad feeling came over me.

I had no choice but to settle this as quickly as possible and posed the question straight out, "Could we stay?" He said he needed to check with his roommate. What? We drove the whole way out there and the roommate decided our fate! I was definitely wrong about my friend and when the roommate said no, our decision was made for us so we headed back to Wichita, Kansas.

Once there, our new plan was to get some crack. We visited the dealer who was always willing to trade off merchandise for crack. We pulled up to his apartment about two o'clock in the morning and we were in luck. His lights were still on and there were people moving all around, as if there was a party going on. Mistake, Mistake, Mistake! My first one was getting out of the car, my next one was forgetting to lock the doors behind me, which was something that Princess D always preached about, and my last mistake was leaving Princess D alone to go off and trade a new camcorder.

I was invited in, as usual, yet from the very start I could tell something strange was going on. This guy ushered me into the bedroom and told me to wait, something that had never been done in the past. Then, out of nowhere, one of the drunken friends came storming into the room and tried to take the camcorder. We tussled, but before an all-out brawl could occur, the dealer came back in and broke us up.

The dealer cursed out his friend, claiming that I was a customer and there as his guest, but his friend was hot and upset with the situation and stormed out. At that point, the only thing that was on my mind was to get what I came for and get out of there. Then I heard the guy and his crew head down the fire escape…the same one I had used to enter the dealer's apartment. My mind was cloudy from all the commotion and I did not remember that those same steps led right back to our car where Princess D was.

When it hit me, I ran out the door and down the fire escape, leaving the camcorder and the dealer behind. But it was too late! As soon as I hit the night air, I knew the situation was not good when I heard the sweet voice of my dear Princess D yell out to me. "BABE!"

One word, and the tone in which she yelled it, demanded my immediate attention and I sprung into action like superman. I leapt down into the midst of what was already a mess - which was a free-for-all out of the backseat of the Olds. Like a pack of hungry wolves, these four guys attacked our loaded car and pulled out whatever they could grab. I was no match for the foursome, but thankful that no fist were thrown and no swings were exchanged. They just grabbed what they had and ran for their cars.

However, there was a much larger problem when Princess D yelled again, "Babe, they got the 'bible'!" These guys had the suitcase with all our identification, equipment and checks – everything we needed to continue our life of crime. As far as I was concerned, that suitcase was worth fighting for, because without it we were lost.

Before I could get too close, one of them stepped up and pulled out a gun, which caused me to have second thoughts. I pleaded with them to give back the suitcase because it had everything we needed for the future; that plea definitely backfired. It encouraged them to keep it, as if they had hit the million dollar lottery. All I could do was stand there and watch as they pulled away into the misty night. I put our things back into the car and locked the doors.

I went straight back into the dealer's apartment, only this time I was not a happy camper. All my anger was directed towards him and I told him that he needed to contact his friends and get my things back. He mentioned his friends belonged to a gang and he highly recommended that I leave it alone. He proceeded to give me what I had initially come for...the crack. I knew the only reason he mentioned this was to deter me from pursuing any recourse.

Deep inside, I was flaming mad and I knew that the dealer was not on the level. He was not about to give me any information that was going to help either. It did not matter though because I had already decided in my mind that I was going to set his apartment complex on fire and burn this guy and all his things to a crisp.

Well, we left with some crack and no direction about what to do or where to go next. Princess D was clearly upset about the whole incident and asked me what we were going to do. It was late – more like really early the next morning – so we headed back to the hotel we had stayed at a few days earlier.

When we got there, I told the office manager we had just been robbed and I needed his help to get a room. I just needed him to put us up until the stores opened and I could get my hands on some cash. I promised to pay for the room first thing in the morning, and we were blessed when the manager extended us that simple kindness.

That morning, I left Princess D behind and went on a mission. I took the only things left with me and headed out of the door – one pen, one set of ID and one checkbook, coupled with my gift of gab. I stopped at a bagel shop and ordered an assortment of bagels for sixty dollars. I handed the cashier a personal check in the amount of two-hundred fifty dollars and received my bagels and change. I took out a few bagels for us and gave the rest to the hotel for extending us a night's stay. After settling the bill with them, I paid for an additional night and headed right upstairs to Princess D.

My life was consumed with this negative lifestyle; I began to hate the way I was living. As a result, I started to take my frustrations out on the person closest to me…Princess D. Instead of smoking crack and enjoying myself, I began to waste the product by burning it up like a chain smoker.

One right after the next, I put fire to the crack, sometimes without inhaling. In turn, I became mean-spirited to Princess D. I was selfish, taking control of everything, and resentful towards her, as if she was to blame for all my problems.

I recall taking the last bottle of scotch we had left and, for no good reason, poured it down the drain. Alcohol was the only thing that kept me level and I had gotten rid of it. I was not a big weed smoker, but after showing off with the scotch deal, Princess D fixed me – she helped me smoke so much weed that I passed out. She knew that I could not handle it and, in her own way, wanted to teach me a lesson.

After checking out of the hotel, we headed to a town in Reno County Kansas called Hutchinson. It was there that the madness continued. After busting a few checks at the local mall, we spotted a hotel directly across the street. We were both tired, so when Princess D suggested we check in, I definitely agreed.

On our way there, I spotted a few guys working on the highway clean-up crew and it did not take me long to realize they were inmates from a prison. Their bright orange suits gave them away and, even though they were still locked up to some extent, they seemed happy to be outside the prison walls and enjoying limited freedom. Deep in my spirit, I knew that this was a sign and that little voice inside my head tried desperately to say something to me, but I would not let it. I refused to listen to reason.

Princess D and I unloaded the car and made ourselves at home in the room, and then we passed out on the bed. An hour later, I woke up and headed to the bathroom for a shower when something amazing and frightening happened.

I stopped and looked in the mirror and, as I gazed at it, I was stunned by what I saw. I did not recognize the person who stood before me. It was as though a complete stranger was staring back at me. All this time, I had been running and chasing that high that I never took time to look at me. I mean I never took time to see who Ronald James had become.

Sure, the mirror showed me my unkempt, tattered hair that was turning gray, my beard that was wolfing, and my skin's complexion that was fading. However, what it revealed when I looked deeper into the reflection was the lost little boy who refused to grow up, someone who was so selfish that he was willing to steal from his own mother.

I was pitiful, a loser. I had become sinful, evil, wicked, and immoral. I was despised, hated by people who once called me their friend. I had become less than nothing, feeling guilt and shame for my actions, and that revelation poured out of that mirror and into my soul.

As my inner self was exposed for what it truly was, it was like a city fire hydrant burst forth with reality. However, my understanding of it was roughly the size of a tea cup! I stood there trying to catch it all, but it was too much. I was overwhelmed. I clinched my fist and gritted my teeth in anger. I cursed the person who stood before me. I hated him and I wanted him gone.

I began a frantic search in our travel bag and finally pulled out a new pack of razors, some shaving gel, and an attitude. Standing at the sink, still glued to the image in the mirror, I turned the hot water on full blast because I wanted to make sure it scalded away the shell of the man that I saw…and gave way to the rebirth of the man I was supposed to be. If I could get rid of him, maybe my life would find new direction.

I proceeded by shaving off my beard and then my moustache, which cleaned my upper lip. I wiped away the steam from the mirror, but he was still there! Frustrated, I shaved my head bald, only to clean the mirror once again and still he was staring back at me. I hated him and I wanted…no, I needed to shed him. I no longer wanted to see this person. Then I went for my eyebrows because I was that desperate, only to realize that no matter what I did to my outer self, my inner self would always reveal its ugly face.

Feeling defeated, disorientated and dismal, I dropped everything. My arms collapsed to their sides and I began to tear up with no expression on my face. The whimper started out as an inner echo in my soul and, when I was done, the cries of all my pain were unleashed.

I dropped to the floor, slumped over my knees, sobbed uncontrollably and called out to God for help. I had laid on the floor of that bathroom in a fetal position for over an hour, crying my heart out, begging God to change me. I needed His help; all the years of running and denying could not hide now.

When I got up, I cannot say that I felt any major changes other than being tired. I finished cleaning myself up, grabbed an ice-cold beer and sat on the edge of the bed. I looked over at Princess D, who was still sound asleep, and wondered why she was still with me when I was so broken.

Then I focused on the television and the 1996 Summer Olympic Games were on. As I watched the track and field events, I noticed something out of the corner of my eye. I saw the shadow of someone outside the hotel window, as if he or she were peeking in. I refused to follow my first instinct, which was to investigate, and figured it was someone from the hotel grounds crew cutting grass.

Then our hotel phone rang so I walked over, picked it up, but heard nothing on the other end, and that seemed strange to me. I know Princess D called the front desk for a wakeup call, but that was not until the following morning.

Without another thought, I blew that off as the hotel's mistake and got back into bed with Princess D. We spent the remaining time cuddled up together and I tried to put out of my mind what had happened earlier.

Later that evening, we were awakened by the sound of someone pounding on our room door. Little did I know my help had arrived. God had heard my distressful cry and sent the Reno County Kansas Police to the rescue. They were in full force, but they were not alone; state and local detectives accompanied them. It took a while for me to open the door because Princess D and I scrambled to hide the checks, ID's and the weed.

It was time to get off this ride so after a number of questions, I gave them my real name and told them Princess

D had nothing to do with this; she was just along for the ride. They said that would not fly as they considered her an accomplice and that she would be dealt with accordingly. Even though Princess D had been through the system before, I still felt horrible bringing her down with me.

Once again, my selfish lifestyle took the freedom of another person. I was taken to and locked up in the Reno County Jail in Kansas. I had to admit that this song and dance was getting old and I was growing tired of it!

When I woke up the following morning in a holding cell, I heard a familiar cry from the holding cell that was next to me…it was Princess D. The police did not buy her story or mine. They knew all about Princess D's involvement and even told me they were sure that the Feds were going to pick up our charges because they had followed our paper trail from Pennsylvania to Kansas.

Our description was easy to follow, and because of it, the police said I was looking at a very, very long stretch of jail time, not to mention that the Pennsylvania Board of Probation and Parole had lodged a detainer on me. I was told that with my record, I was done – yes, you could stick a fork in me!

There I was in the heart of Kansas, with who knows how many charges on me, my car impounded, the Feds knocking on my cell door, but the worst part was that my actions caused my friend, Princess D, to be dragged down as well. Why did God allow this to happen? I thought He loved me, and then it hit me…HE DID love me…and still does regardless of what I have done.

The course of events that led up to our arrest actually spared us true hardship. The suitcase that we called our 'bible' had been taken away and, as a result, there was very little the police had to go on, so consequently, the Feds never did pick up our case.

Yes, God had heard my cry and sent me help within a few hours. I had no idea that His help would have been in the form of silver bracelets. Did God put me in jail? No, my actions and poor choices led me to prison; however, God had mercy on me in a number of ways throughout a number of events. He knew which way I was going even before I did.

Princess D and I were split up and sent to the female/male sections of the prison. We were able to communicate through my mother, MiMi, and we managed to send letters to each other. In one of those letters, I mustered up the humility to apologize for what occurred. I also found the courage, even though I was scared to death, to ask her if she would still marry me. I sent the letter off, not knowing when, or if, I would get a response considering the situation I had put her in. When I called home, my mom shared the good news with me – Princess D had said YES!

In order to hurry things along at the prison, we both copped out to a plea, which was a blessing for us and we could move forwards with our lives. We were offered 2 years of probation. Our public defender told us that the detectives felt we had bigger charges to face in Pennsylvania; that is why they were willing to settle with the plea in exchange for our speedy exit back to Pennsylvania.

Princess D and I went through the courts of Kansas with our public defenders; we were able to arrange for our sentencing and our wedding to fall on the same day before the same judge. There was a certain buzz among the staff, and we were the talk of the jail. It was an exciting event to them. No one had ever done what we were about to do.

Our sentencing day finally came and we were ushered

into the courthouse from the prison. We went before Judge Becker and he was very straight forward, yet fair. After a stern talking to, he sentenced us both to the 2 year plea agreement. He made it clear that I was going to be held in Reno County on my parole detainer until I could be extradited back to Pennsylvania. However, Princess D was free to go on her own and just needed to report to county probation once she got back to Pennsylvania.

Judge Becker continued with the marriage ceremony and declared us husband and wife. We smiled at each other and finally kissed. That was a special moment and I had a good feeling about our lives together.

Two things about prisons – they may claim they are overcrowded, but they will always manage to find room, and it is easy to get in but hard to get out. I believe it was October 15, 1996 when I walked back into SCI Graterford with, once again, a string of charges to my name and plenty of questions to answer.

Uwchland Township Police Department: charged with theft by deception, receiving stolen, property, forgery, and bad checks;

Ambler Police Department and Upper Dublin Township: charged with theft by deception, receiving stolen property, forgery, and bad checks;

Whipanin Township Police Department: charged with theft by deception, receiving stolen property, forgery, bad checks and theft by unlawful taking or dispose;

Towamencin Township Police Department: charged with theft by deception receiving stolen property, forgery, and bad checks;

Malvern Police Department: charged with theft by

deception and 2 cases each of receiving stolen property and forgery.

All in all, and as I said earlier, it was the same old song and dance, plus I had violated my state parole and ended back Upstate. There, I found myself back at church, but this time I wanted to give God my all and I knew I had to mean it, live it and not stray from it. I was determined to make a change; however, my change ended up pushing Princess D away from me.

When I realized it and tried to fix it, things were too far gone. She had tried a few visits and phone calls, but the super selfish Christian…me, myself and I…Ronald James, had a different plan, and our communication came to a close… as did the good feeling about our lives together. I did not recognize the type of emotion I was really working with, so I tucked away this feeling of resentment that was spelled D-I-V-O-R-C-E.

It was time to go home in September of 1999, and I recall everyone in the prison had talked about Y2K and the problems it intended to bring. It had been all over the news and in the papers. Most people thought that the world would come to an end, or at least all the computers would crash. I could not be concerned about that and had centered all my energy toward rebuilding my life.

My sister, Lori, came that day to pick me up. As I stood outside the prison walls at SCI Graterford, with my box of personal belongings in hand, I had the penitentiary glow and wore a gigantic smile. My sister had a lot of faith in me and she was very confident that this would be my last bout with incarceration.

"Commit a crime and the world is made of glass"

-Ralph Waldo Emerson

CHOICE SEVEN
LATANYA

FOR THE NEXT SEVERAL months I was a stand-up person in the community. I attended church and helped people whenever I could. I had landed a decent job and been promoted several times. I found a new woman with whom I built a relationship, I was clean, and I even walked off my parole and probation with minor difficulty. Princess D and I had finalized our divorce and moved on as friends. I was encouraged and supported by pastors from the state of Kansas, Illinois and Pennsylvania, and I had chaplains, employers, attorneys, friends and family all standing beside me.

With a full head of steam, I moved forward with my life and on New Year's Eve 1999, I got engaged to a beautiful young woman by the name of Latanya Moore, and took on the responsibility of her three adorable children.

Then on September 2, 2000, I tied the knot for the third time. Wait, hold on one freaking minute…something is wrong with this story! Yes, you are right. Even though I just shared that my divorce with Princess D was final, I was still married. If you did not catch it, I, Ronald James was still married to Cheryl!

Our wedding was very nice although, when the preacher held up our wedding bands, he asked a simple question

"Is there any reason why these two people should not be married?" That voice inside me that was usually very subtle was now screaming 'DO NOT DO THIS RONALD JAMES! YOU ARE ALREADY MARRIED TO CHERYL! WALK AWAY! RUN AWAY, RON…NOW! However, I was too selfish and proud to listen, so I just ignored it.

Marriage has ways of changing people. Usually you work together and build a life of happy memories. However, time away from prison and marriage brought out the selfish old me, and even though my beautiful wife was now pregnant with our child, it did not matter to me. I had decided to embark on a selfish rampage and was about to put her and the children through hell. I mean pure, unadulterated hell, and I am almost certain that if she were to write a book on this topic, it would be titled I Married a Monster!

Straight to the point, I stole from Latanya, and I am not talking just a television like I stole from my mother. I stole everything and anything that I could pawn for drugs – her pocketbooks, shoes, jewelry, cash, even her clothes…you name it, I stole it.

I stole her phones and smashed them because I thought she was having an affair. I stole the family computer from the children, their video games and believe it or not, I stole food out of the freezer. I later stole our car and rented it out to drug dealers.

I also would joy ride with my fellow crack heads and hoes and, if that was not enough, I smashed the car's windshield, broke the steering column and stunk it up with my crack funk. I came in the house at all hours of the night, disturbed her sleep and accused her of cheating, only because I was and it was easier to blame her rather than taking responsibility for my own actions.

I tormented her at work by calling numerous times each day and playing all kinds of head games. I also had women call her just to antagonize her. I forced myself on her sexually and smoked crack in the basement, in our bedroom, and then I did it anywhere in the house whenever I wanted.

I argued her down, belittled her, cursed her out and lied to her. One night, I ran out of the house like a mad man with her pocketbook, wearing only a pair of sweatpants. On my way out of the door, the only thing that slowed me down was that she tried to hang on me. I managed to push her to the floor, pregnant and all, and when I got outside, I ran like hell because I knew the police were coming.

I finally stopped running that night only because I fell off a 2-story high water main pipe. My loving wife still tried to make things work. She even picked me up later that night and took me to the hospital for my injuries, only having to admit herself as a patient because of stress. It was because of the grace of God that she did not miscarry. If she had, this would be a totally different chapter of my life and I doubt it would have had the same ending.

She finally separated from me because I had truly abandoned her and the children. In the process, she also placed a restraining order against me, which I violated more than a few times. I was crazed and did all kinds of nasty things to her, like stealing her trash just to go through it to see what I could dig up on her.

On those very few and rare occasions when we got back together and tried to make the marriage work, I did all those same things over again. I had not stopped my antics and I think I was even crazier than before, so when she finally had enough, we separated again. Only this time, I stopped paying the mortgage on the house because I had lost both of my jobs, so this forced my family out into the streets.

Everything I did to this sweet woman and those innocent children was extremely unfair, including how I tried to control our finances and when she could see her own relatives. I was obnoxious and downright nasty to her, her friends and her family.

At times for no good reason, I had hatred in my heart towards some of them. I am certain the mental damage I caused Latanya was, by far, worse than any of the physical or material damage I caused during our time together. She really wanted our marriage to work and I was just too ridiculous at that time to figure it out.

One night after running in and out the house multiple times, she begged me to stay. She had tears in her eyes and cried out, "Ron, please stay", hugging and kissing me, stepping backwards to lay herself across our bed, pulling off her clothes for me to make love to her…pleading with me to be with her. I looked at my wife who was spread like an eagle and then at the door. I turned back to her with my cash in hand and said, "I'll be back."

I am convinced she was devastated as she watched me turn and walk out the door to the streets. You cannot imagine the abuse I put this poor woman, her family and our daughter through. I am ashamed, and I am sharing all of this because the world needs to know that my loving ex-wife Latanya did all she could to make our marriage work. I did nothing to be the true man of the household and just continued with one bad, selfish choice after another. Following a bitter divorce, God only knows why she remained a supportive friend to me, but I am thankful and grateful.

I would like to drive this point home. My selfish choices

took me farther than I wanted to go. It cost me more than I was willing to pay and kept me longer then I wanted to stay. Would this ever end? Once again, I had jumped on the crazy train headed for nowhere.

CHOICE EIGHT
ME, MYSELF AND I ...AGAIN

I HAD WANTED TO explore some new areas so I made a brief tour of Washington, DC, but landed back in Kansas. I had already done so much damage in Wichita that I was certain my photo was on every community service board at every store entrance with a caption in large, very bold print 'Wanted for passing bad checks'. This only confirms my level of self-centeredness, as if the world revolved around Ronald James and I was that great check-writing scam artist who was being hunted down.

A friend decided to take me out on a shopping run on Black Friday and we ended up getting busted in Harvey County, Kansas. Doom and gloom set in as the police intercom blared and told me to step out of the truck and put my hands where they could be seen. There were at least five police cars, all parked facing our truck, all with their driver's door opened, all the officers standing at the ready, and I thought to myself, "fine mess you are in once again, Ron James!". As the officers shouted again for me to lift both my hands over my head, I looked down at my shirt and wondered what all those small red lights centered on my chest were? "Hey people, what the hell is going on here? It is not like I killed anyone...I just posted a bad check!"

As I walked backwards, I was ever so careful because I did not want to stumble over my own two feet. If I did, I believe these yahoos would have mistaken my movements for something else and opened fire on me!

Unbelievable – I had only passed one bad check at the local Dairy Queen for one-hundred dollars; the other two places did not go for my 'take a personal check that I claimed was a traveler's check' scam.

So there I was, locked up in Harvey County, Kansas with nothing to my name except another lists of charges and a two-hundred eighty dollars bail. No big deal you say, but it was a very big deal when you have burned all your bridges and you do not have any money, so I settled in.

There was something very amazing about getting locked up. After it happened, I always thought of the 'I wish I could have' or the 'Man, I should have' or the 'if only I would have' statements; however, there was something else that took place right after the shock of getting caught.

It was, and still is, called the window of opportunity for the surrender. That window was short-lived, was always followed by self-pity, and then concluded with some form of resentment towards self, someone or something else. The reality hits you and all you could think about was that you had to get out of that place if it was the last thing you did. For me, it almost became like a chess game.

Harvey County's bail was set up like this – no matter what your bail was, and in order to be released on bail, you needed someone to co-sign for you. With no cell phone in my possession, I was without any possible leads or phone numbers to call, and the few numbers I could remember were to my cousin Peanut - who was still upset with me, and a handful of drug dealers - who would have loved to hear from me. It definitely felt like checkmate with so little to go on, so my next move was to form an alliance with someone from jail.

For the most part, I was a walking victim (vick) and I was willing to do almost anything to get out of jail. Now if larceny was in your heart, which it was in mine, it was that easy for you to be taken advantage of and made into a vick.

I looked for anyone who would listen to my cry and every time I spoke to someone, it was about my situation. That was when I finally met Mr. Match. I called him that because he was truly my match. He eased his way in, he listened to my cry, and then he came on strong with a solution for me. He offered to have his wife co-sign on my behalf so I could get out.

Rule number one: if it sounds too good to be true, it usually is! However, I was so desperate that I had never considered Mr. Match could have played me.

Long story short, I had my sister wire my entire unemployment benefit check to his wife, which was for eight-hundred dollars. The deal was I paid the bail money plus two-hundred dollars to his wife for her part in the deal, and the rest would go towards rent after they invited me to stay at their house.

It was clear that Mr. Match did not want me to jump bail – he drove that point home! It would just be easier for his wife to keep an eye on me if I stayed at his place. He also told me his wife was no joke and I had better fly right when I got there. I agreed and the deal was done…well at least on my end.

After the money was picked up, I was told I needed to wait until his wife would come and get me. This, of course, never happened and you probably figured out that part of the story by now…I, however, did not get it as quickly.

I waited two days, then a week, and then by the end of second week, reality set in and it became apparent I had been taken for a fool. What was my next move? I was hot and going to take a section out of his head! All my mouthing off about how I was going to fix that guy got me moved off the block. How could that guy set me up like that and get away with my eight-hundred dollars? What gave him the right to steal from me? Who was he to con me? I felt violated, embarrassed and full of rage and resentment…and I wanted blood! Notice again that I refused to take responsibility for any part!

It was no fun when the bear had the gun. I hate to say it, but I was experiencing only a tidbit of what I had dished out to hundreds of other unsuspecting people on a regular basis. Who was I to think that I was beyond being taken? For the most part, I had lost out on most of my life because of my own choices, so I had no one to blame but myself.

I took my licks and worked another angle. I really wanted my life to fall back in line with good morals and proper living; however, I was beat up and had lost so much that I was not ready to give God the one thing he wanted – death of myself. I held onto Ronald James with all my strength and I was far from letting go. I was so selfish that I held on to the very thing that was required of me in order for me to live.

By holding on to Ronald James, I was killing him. All I needed to do was surrender me, but yours truly foiled all my good intentions and positive plans to live my life finally and fully for Jesus.

Having several days to think about what to do next, I made a few phone calls; I felt optimistic that I would be bailed out. I had the bail bond company call a friend who told them everything they wanted to hear, and the following day I was called to the Intake office so the bondsman could sign me out. I loved it when a plan came together…or did it? Just as

I thought the door to freedom had been opened, it seemed yet again that my past had come back to haunt me.

It was in Pennsylvania where the National Crime Information Center (NCIC) noticed my activity in the state of Kansas. I had a number of open check charges with both Chester and Montgomery Counties in Pennsylvania, but nothing that they were willing to pursue individually. They began to work collectively with Kansas and agreed to extradite me back to Pennsylvania. It was my luck that what could go wrong, just went wrong. I was kept in a holding cell because apparently Harvey County Jail in Kansas was waiting for a phone call from Pennsylvania as to whether to hold me or let me go.

I then asked the officer if I could make a phone call to at least let my friends know what was going on. They granted my request and I was grateful to find out my friends were still coming to pick me up. I sat in that holding cell for another hour before I came up with an idea...Hey, that was what think tanks were made for, right?

I asked the jailer, who was an older, stern-looking white woman, if I could use the phone one more time, claiming that I had been unable to connect with my friends about picking me up. She agreed and once I got on the phone, I simply called the prison. You read that correctly! I called the very jail I was in and spoke with the stern jailer.

As we talked, I could see her behind the glass. All I said was, "Yes, this is detective such and such from the State of Pennsylvania, we have no need for Ronald James and you can cut him loose or do whatever you were going to do with him. Thanks."

Before I could hang up the receiver, the jailer was yelling for me to get off the phone. She told me what I already knew and wanted to hear. "James, Pennsylvania does not need you so let's get you out of here." Well...I signed out, paid my bail, was given my cash, and I was off to the races once again. Yes, I had escaped! However, what I really needed to escape from was myself. Ronald James was not going anywhere except back to jail.

Two weeks after my great escape, I found myself back for the third time in the Sedgwick County Prison...this time for forgery. The two prior visits were for retail theft and drug possession, and both times I was released the following day.

So there I was in another jail, in another holding tank, and once again felt sorry for myself. However, the God of understanding was right there for me, but I still was oblivious to what I needed to do.

I never really had the chance to settle in at Sedgwick County Prison. Before I knew it, I was being shuffled down to Intake to be processed out of their prison. Since I had already been there and done that with this prison twice before, I knew the drill and I thought the Transcore was there to extradite me back to Pennsylvania. However, things were different this time.

I was ushered onto a plane and accompanied by two detectives – one from Chester County and the other from Montgomery County – and before I knew it, I was right back smack in the middle of Chester County Prison Farms.

Why did I continue to subject myself to this vicious cycle of pain, hand cuffs, shackles, fear of the unknown, holding tanks, hundreds of questions, stripped searched, photographed, finger printed, bail hearings, arraignments, pre-trial conferences, lawyers, public defenders, judges, sheriffs, more isolation, cell mates, inmates with masks, correctional officers and guards with attitudes, living in a bathroom with another man, sleeping on a two-inch thick mattress and more and more questions…and that was just for starters?!

As in my past, I found myself carted in and out of prison with what seemed like a daily string of new charges. It seemed as if everyone wanted a piece of me and I found myself in the Court of Chester County with the following charges:

Easttown Township Police Department: charged with theft by unlawful taking or dispose, theft of services, identity theft, unlawful device-making equipment, and forgery. I was then carted off to the awaiting arms of the Towamencin Township Police Department: For their convenience and mine, they asked me to work with them and, if I would agree to waive all hearings to the higher courts, they would consolidate all my cases. That meant I would only have to appear in front of one judge for four different Montgomery County Townships and all their charges. I agreed and it went something like this:

Towamencin Township Police Department: charged with theft by deception, receiving stolen property, forgery, bad checks, and identity theft.

Lower Providence Township Police Department: charged with 3 counts of forgery, 2 counts of bad checks, theft by deception, receiving stolen property, and identity theft.

Montgomery Township Police Department: charged with receiving stolen property, 2 counts of bad checks, and 3 counts of theft by deception.

Whitpain Township Police Department: charged with 2 counts of forgery, theft by unlawful taking or dispose, theft by deception, receiving stolen property, bad checks, and identity theft.

The Towamencin Police Detective was so pleased with

how things went that he offered to treat me to a free lunch. Know this people…Nothing is free when it is being offered by an officer of the system to a prisoner in handcuffs!

He asked me, "How about a tasty, juicy Philly cheesesteak, James?" I quickly said, "Sure." He continued with "What about a soda, too?" I did not hesitate with a "Yes Sir and make it a Coke."

Normally, I would have expected to eat any meal in the confines of a holding cell, alone, or with the others who are also in the tank, but for some reason, my lunch was brought to me and I was able to eat right in front of the other police and detectives.

It did not dawn on me that anything was wrong, that they were up to something, that I had been played…that was until about half-way through my sandwich the officer asked, "James, how is that sandwich tasting?" I claimed that it was good, but the sandwich was average at best and it did had a funny taste. However, I knew it took many things working together to pull off a great Philly cheesesteak, so I figured it was an average shop where the police had always purchased lunch.

The officer continued to share information with me and said, "James, you know this cheesesteak sandwich came from the pizza shop that you ripped off with those bad checks?" By this time, I had taken another bite and thought to myself what could be the reason he was telling me this.

Well…as I looked at the detective and at the other officers who sat around the table, they had all begun to snicker and laugh. I got my answer with only a fourth of the sandwich left. It hit me that something was wrong with my sandwich and when I opened it up to investigate…oh no, they did NOT just do that!

I cannot say with one-hundred percent certainty, but in my opinion, what I saw when I opened the sandwich appeared to be shit…dog shit or cat shit I do not know, but either way it was shit…in my sandwich…that I had just eaten!

No wonder it was free! No wonder they were laughing!! My insides began to turn, but I held my composure. I was not about to let them see me sweat and I certainly was not going to hurl, although that would have been an even exchange as far as I was concerned.

Overall, I guess I deserved that cruel trick, and I had to compare this incident with the perspective of jail life in that they were pretty much the same. You always had to watch what you said or did to someone because if they did not like it, you could definitely count on a crapload of paybacks…no pun intended!

I did my time at Chester County and on May 5, 2004 I moved on to complete my detainer at Montgomery County.

<u>Upper Gwynedd Township Police Department</u>: charged with receiving stolen property, criminal conspiracy, burglary, 2 counts of possessing an instrument of crime, prohibited offensive weapons, theft by extortion, intimidation of witness/victim, theft by deception, criminal attempt theft by deception, and criminal attempt theft by unlawful taking or dispose. It seemed as if they charged me with everything but the kitchen sink.

On October 16, 2005, I finished my detainer at Montgomery County and transferred to Hershey, Pennsylvania, also known as Chocolatetown USA…the sweetest place on earth. You would think there would be free access to all the Hershey Kisses I would want, but not exactly and that was a disappointment since I love chocolate.

I arrived there to enter a drug and alcohol rehab program

at Conowago Place in hopes of finally breaking my drug habit. I completed the scheduled program and then transferred to the Gate House for Men, a halfway house in Lititz, Pennsylvania. I was there a few months and thought I had my act my together…at least I acted that way…so they granted my release and I was back out into the world. Unfortunately, with or without rehab, I was left to my own devices and, as you have read, that was never a good thing. Within months, I relapsed.

It was November 17, 2006 when Manheim Township Police Department booked me on relatively simple charges of depositing an empty envelope into my bank's checking account with the intention of withdrawing money that was not there.

After the booking process, I was taken to Lancaster County Prison where I tried to get someone to post bail for me, but I was finally out of resources. I had done far too much damage for anyone to reach out to me.

So there I sat; it gave Montgomery County time to work through all the paperwork and, within a week, they filed a number of new violations against me. Things looked something like this:

Manheim Township Police Department: charged with theft by deception and 2 charges each of criminal attempt theft by deception and criminal attempt theft by unlawful taking or dispose. Additional charges added were 2 charges each of forgery and criminal attempt theft by deception, 5 charges each of identity theft and 10 charges each of criminal conspiracy of identity theft.

Warwick Township Police Department: charged with theft by unlawful taking or dispose, forgery, and theft by deception.

Lancaster Police Department: sealed the deal with new charges of insurance fraud, unsworn falsification to authorities, false reports to law enforcement, and last but not least, Montgomery County added 4 separate violations of pretty much the same description. My criminal run and lifestyle had finally come to an end. After about a week of incarceration, I realized I was not going anywhere any time soon. I was in this for the long haul.

"If others learn from our mistakes and it saves them from the pain that we ourselves experienced, then it wasn't all in vain.

-Our Daily Bread 3/15/12

CHOICE NINE
THE KING

KING?…YES, KING…SO ACT LIKE one and live like one. This shout is heard loud and clear every day in my soul. After the run I had, you would think it was about time I started living like one. It took me a long time and many choices to get to this stage of the game, but I finally made it.

May 14, 2012 I was released from prison. You may ask yourself, 'where is Ron James now? Has he fallen back to his old ways as every time before and gotten caught up in drugs once again?' Well, I hate to disappoint you, but the real story of my life is just beginning! My life since that day can best be summed up by the song "Changed" by Rascal Flatts:

> 'Could finally see where I was going
> I'm not the same man I was then
> I hit my knees, now here I stand
> There I was, now here I am Changed'

Since my release, I have not had an alcoholic drink, I have not sought after, chased after or wanted after drugs of any sort. I have not seen the likes of a traffic cop, an Intake officer or an inmate guard…or the insides of any police station or prison for that matter.

I have secured a job with an international franchise organization and have been promoted to director of a call center within that organization. I have experienced the joy of honestly and legally obtaining and paying for an apartment and a new car. I am involved with Toastmasters International and have been a featured speaker at many events, even won several competitions, and have been elected president of our local group.

I have a wonderful woman by my side who knows my story and accepts me for who I am today, and wants to be with me for the rest of her life! In fact, we were married September 21, 2013!

I have also received good news …no, great news from the Parole Office – I have been released from Department of Corrections and no longer must report daily to them. I am free to live my life, in my own apartment, doing works for God and my neighbors every day! I am truly blessed and grateful to all those who spoke on my behalf and had a part in making this parole happen.

I want to live like a king…The King…every day of my life for the rest of my life, and that is all I want for you, too. The choices you make will allow that if you only let them.

America the beautiful, land of opportunity to everyone, and those fortunate enough to work in the greatest country in the world know that the American dream is afforded to all. Part of that dream is to be financially independent and that is achieved in a number of ways.

Owning your own business, in my opinion, would be the easiest way to achieve the windfall of success. My dream was to be successful by way of the King Pin status. Others of you may prefer the words boss, CEO, President or Founder, but for my analogy, let us play with the word King Pin. Well, maybe just the word 'king' since the owner is technically the king of his business.

It is his responsibility to make sure things are operational and run with synergy. A king needs a kingdom to conduct his affairs…surely, what good would a king be without a kingdom? If he is without dominion, he is without rule and his authority is pointless, his commands meaningless. He would be sovereign over his own shadow and that was only when the sun was shining. There is something embedded deep within each of us that drives us to want to be king and in control of, if nothing else, his or her own life.

For my example, use your imagination and share with me the image of the chessboard. It seems fitting to use this as a comparison since you definitely find a king there. The game of chess consist of thirty-two pieces, sixteen for each player and, of course, each side has a king, his queen, two rooks, two knights, two castles, and eight pawns.

Foolishly, most argue that the queen is the most important piece on the board because of her mobility, which they interpret as power. However, the queen actually has less value than the king, and the game can continue without her.

In contrast, the game ceases without the king; therefore, he would be considered the most important piece on the board.

Strategically, the game has many facets; however, it is set up for one side to ultimately conquer and take down the king of the opposing side. In order for the king to survive and remain standing, all pieces are subjects of play. This also includes the sacrificing of the queen, if necessary.

If you have never played the game, I will try to provide you a better understanding of the game. If you have engaged in the game or act of warfare (chess), you know that making your next move your best move is the way to stay ahead and win the game. I say this because most people who play chess know what it is like to win. The king understands winning because winning is the only name of the game for him.

Now let us use our imaginations once again and look at life as being this great big chessboard. Better yet, let us go a step deeper and consider life as an unlimited number of chessboards that each person has to play on.

As a person moves throughout their life, they find themselves on a number of boards we will call daily life. Each person has a choice to play on any of the boards he or she chooses. Some of the boards have titles to help with your selection, but by no means are representative of all of life's opportunities.

Being a father to your children, a productive parent, a role model in and around your community, staying in school, graduating high school, advancing to college, starting a career, serving in our armed forces, getting married, having children, investing, creating and inventing things, owning your own business, playing sports, being an artist, singer or painter. These are all options available to every one of us every day. Which do you choose? With so many out there, how do you begin to make these choices?

Then there is the other side, the immoral side with a number of boards to play on as well. The streets, prostitution, pimping, running games (con), gang violence, selling drugs, robbing, shootings, inside trading, embezzlement, retail theft, identity theft, employer theft of hours or merchandise…The list could go on, but you get my point.

Some may say the hand they were dealt in life was not a fair hand and that is the only board they have to play on. In addition, there are an infinite number of factors that could aid or prevent them doing any of the things listed above – pro, con or both. A person's wealth, environment, social class, status, upbringing, culture, abilities and a host of other things could be factors in the game, depending on the board you chose. However, free will is YOUR choice, coupled with God's will in all.

My main thought here is to express the fact that if we tap into all of our creative abilities, resources and passions that drive us, while recognizing God's purpose for our lives, we can live our lives as kings and play on the only board that matters.

That means putting away sin and iniquity, along with our selfish desires to serve flesh with the lust that the world has to offer, and do what is right for the right reasons. For me, that means serving others, for true kings do whatever they can to take care of their kingdoms. They look to help others and ultimately glorify the King of Kings, (Matthew 22:37). Therefore, a king is only a king when he truly believes and glorifies the King.

I finally surrendered to self and made the choice to glorify God. I have made my next move my best move and that is to serve you. Anyone who is willing to look at not only my past life of bad choices, but themselves and those around them, with forgiveness and grace will become the king you have been called to become.

There are countless boards to choose from, but once you choose to play for the King of Kings, you will win! The board I chose to play on is "Love your neighbor as yourself" (Matthew 22:39) and my choices every day are made around this decision that no one deserves to be treated any less than how I want to be treated. I will pray for any person suffering a hardship, needing blessing, health or emotional support. I will make it my mission to treat every person I meet with respect, whether they deserve it or not, because that is how God loved and how He wants us to love our neighbors.

My mother, MiMi, once said, "Ronnie, you love real hard." What she meant was I have an inner drive, a passion and a determination to press forward to get what I want. It took me a long time to figure this out since the majority of my life had been spent pleasing me. Now that I have surrendered and chosen to play for the King, all that energy will be directed at serving you, my neighbor…World, watch out!

"*I can't change the past, but I am fully responsible for the actions and the choices I make now and in the future and I will make a living restitution.*"

-*Author Unknown*

CHOICE TEN
CONCLUSION OF CHOICES

I DO NOT CLAIM to be a prophet or someone who can read into the future. However, I do believe certain events have happened in my lifetime to set the stage for my awareness, understanding, and clarity of those who are spiritually blind, suffer with addictions, and battle with the issue of self to help them recognize that what they are doing or the way they are living is morally wrong.

When I first began my jail run in Pennsylvania in 1986, I was oblivious to first-hand prison life, but I was not ignorant to the mindsets that were around me – self-centeredness and selfishness. The prisoners' mindset was 'keep to yourself, mind your own business, keep your eyes open, keep your mouth shut and respect others.'

The corrections mindset was 'if a person wants help, we will provide it'. Other than that, the extent of what they provided was that everyone was clothed, well fed and had a place sleep. Once the debt to society was paid, they made sure the person was released. The society's mindset was 'anyone and everyone can make a mistake'.

However, something happened to cause the mindsets of all three systems – prisoner, prison and society – to change. Drugs, mainly cocaine, poured into our streets, our communities and our homes. Once a rich man's high, it had now become available to the average Joe for as little as five – ten dollars. Supply had to keep up with demand and thousands upon thousands of people became drug dealers overnight. Then crack cocaine was introduced and it was a brand new ball game. The drug dealers were already in place to be pawns.

Between heroin, powder cocaine and crack, the media had a field day. They created fear in mainstream America by displaying the crazy actions of the drug user and addict. The politicians and the media painted a picture of an out of control epidemic, resulting in a declaration of the war on drugs. Remember, the government – the same ones who allowed tons of drugs to enter our country – created the war.

Let us stop here for a moment and ponder that comment… is there something going on behind the scenes that we the American people should know about? Why is it that the major players in the drug game, better known as the government, trades arms with countries who mass markets tons of poisons, better known as drugs, that end up flooding our country, streets and neighborhoods?

How is it that these same drugs are made available to an oppressed group of people? The movies and television have created fake role models to mimic? How on earth did Ann Walther, Smith and Western, Colt, Glock, automatic weapons, and a slew of others land in the hands of the same oppressed people? Why did the media scare the living daylights out of main stream America with their constant stories about drug cartels, arms dealing in exchange for drugs, addicts running crazy on the streets?

The politicians declaration of war on drugs created a bunch of pawns fallen on someone else's chessboard. Their declaration created a money need - for more protection from the drug violence and for more prisons to house the offenders of that violence. Why...because the whole drug game was provided by the government, and now it was that same government giving speeches about how bad drugs were and that all the bad people needed to locked up. It became the Us (prisoners) vs. Them (everyone else) game.

In the process, millions became addicted and I am not just talking about drugs. The lifestyle as well; thus creating more jobs for judges, clerks, attorneys, bailiffs, county officers, sheriffs, correctional officers, politicians, detectives, police, public defenders, construction workers to build more prisons, more of everything to process more bad people and so on. A true boost in our economy; however once the prisons grew, the mindsets changed.

The prisoners being locked up were children and teens, and the laws had changed o those youth who were fourteen, fifteen sixteen or seventeen years old are easily certified as adults, classified as major offenders and sent upstate for violent crimes to serve year terms so drastically high they could be numbers you would see at an NBA basketball game.

However, in most cases they were sentenced to life or death. These bitter teens who bought into the lie had no parents, or lack thereof for one reason or another, were resentful and full of rage. In some cases, they tell the courts and their victims to go screw themselves. They have shown little to no respect for authority and have turned the mindset of prison life into an 'F-it' type attitude. All because of selfishness.

The correction's mindset has become strictly about numbers, and any program offered by them is not voluntary and forced upon the inmate, who resents the fact of someone telling him/her what to do. Their parents were not there to tell them so why should they listen to you?

These programs simply do not work, so the correction's main concern became security and babysitting most of the people in jail for a drug related offenses. This, in my opinion, has millions upon millions of taxpayer's dollars being wasted.

The mindset of society has become fear. It is those and them that the fingers are being pointed at. The offender and the felon are treated almost as if they had a deadly disease. No longer are those who fall victim to the system (by choice or chance) looked upon as an everyday US citizen. No, not now, their media image is felon, criminal, ex-offender; A clear separation between classes.

Those with records…us or them, however you want to look at it, the mindset is lock'em up and keep'em locked up, hell…throw away the key.

The future as I see it is hell. If you choose not to believe me, it is not my fault. The mindset of the prisoner sees the injustice, he hears about the injustice, and feels it because he is right in the middle of it. He is defeated, tired, and stuck. His cries are no longer heard, and any attempt to speak up is dealt with using extreme repercussions, as if he was an armed terrorist.

Now, I am not saying there is no hope, no! Hope is what has kept me alive and encouraged me and others in the direction of positive change. What I am saying is the outcome of what I see is modern day slavery, both mind and body.

Prisoners are in a system that they will either conform to or max out of - the years on sentencing will be so high that it will mean a life sentence. Who wants that?

The mindset of the corrections: build new prisons and they will come. New laws will dictate that those who have sex crimes will need to be monitored twenty-four hours a day, seven days a week for life. They will start using a GPS-type chips to track the whereabouts of these offenders. These chips will be imbedded into a person's skin and will be told that it is painless and not a big deal, but in order to be released you will carry this chip so that we can track your every move. This will move to the violent offenders and lastly to all offenders. Your only option will be to accept this device or max out (life sentence)

The prison will accept these newly formed federal or state contracts because of the money that can be generated. The mindset of society will be right in line. Why should we pay for these criminals any longer? They are the other, or separate, class. They harm us, steal from us, break the laws, and burden our tax dollars. The politicians who will seek approval and election or re-election will pass new laws for all people in prison to work camps, factories, industries, on farms, or anywhere else they can profit from the inmates labor.

They will pay each inmate a wage for his or her labor from pennies to a few dollars an hour. Now our great country will be able to compete with Mexico, China, and other foreign countries and their work forces. We will be able to create products at a very low cost, boosting our economy even more.

In addition, for all those illegals who like crossing the border? We got something for you too! Come one, come all! Some might say this will never happen. Well, I hate to break the news to you, but it is already in effect.

You have people who are unemployed, losing their homes and everything they have spent their whole lives to achieve. Gas prices are sky high and the cost of living is up. You have no idea what people will do under pressure and these things and others will only add to the numbers who would normally cope, however now they find themselves in front of a judge, or worse yet…in prison.

Then you will have each state claiming bankruptcy, which forces them to make cuts on every level, and I believe one of these cuts we will see will be to let the prisoners go…but this will be just to activate something that is taking place in the big picture.

When we see this massive movement to free prisoners across the US (state by state), then look for a wave of new crimes that the media will hype up. The fear will move main stream USA to a panic, thus placing pressure on elected officials to seal the deal, which justifies spending for the need of more and more prisons…and it will be this cycle of individuals who will begin working as slaves.

Be forewarned, what sounds like a solution on what to do with ex-offenders will develop into hundreds of slave camps throughout the USA. It is time to wake up, find and accept the purpose for your life, and glorify God.

My last attempt to drive my point home about the future of prison is this: jail is not fun! I see the damage it has caused myself and others. If you are locked up, you risk losing your wealth, health, reputation, position, safety, family, friends and so much more.

No longer are you able to protect the things in life that are important or of value to you. Whatever you have seen portrayed on television about prison life DOES NOT EVEN come close to its reality. It is far worse, and you have no idea how humans can treat or mistreat others; it is unspeakable.

Do not come to jail. If you do, you are in for the long haul. Yes, you who cheats on his taxes; who keeps driving drunk; the person who gives false information to insurance companies; all those who steal from their job; employee theft;

the drug user; the person who places his hands on people; the abusive spouse; the person who says something out of order or threatening a police or law enforcement agent; the drug dealer; shop lifter; sex offender; or any little thing that breaks the law…and buddy, you will find yourself in a prison work camp.

It is time to be set apart and live productive lives to glorify God. Now ask yourself this question, "Do I want to go to jail today?" If you are thinking about doing anything immoral or that would break the law, then ask yourself, Do I want to go to jail today? Your answer is not of importance to me, but your choice is…

ABOUT THE AUTHOR

A SOUGHT-AFTER SPEAKER AND author, Ron James teaches, entertains and inspires audiences of all ages. His Toastmasters International speaking experience provides him with the ability to deliver humorous, yet to-the point presentations. His words make the listener become emotional about what they are hearing, and therefore, think about the circumstances surrounding their own life or the lives of people close to them.

He draws on more than 25 years of experience to teach people how to make better choices. His programs on life events, coupled with a scared-straight approach to the harsh realities of prison, will open your eyes to a place that is becoming easier and easier to get in to, but extremely difficult to get out of. Ron stirs individuals to decide on better, wiser choices for everyday life.

Today, Ron's keynote speeches, seminars, workshops and training events attract many diverse audiences from elementary school students to the 'Big Box' Retail employees and management teams, and from parents to professionals.

His book, CHOICES, was birthed as a way to inspire and help change lives.

Ron lives in the Greater Harrisburg area of Pennsylvania with his wife Annie and their blended families.

If this story has moved or inspired you in any way, let us know. We are here to listen to your stories and share in your life-changing moments because every choice comes with a consequence – we want you to enjoy fully the positive benefits that come with good life choices.

Kriss-Kross.org and Ron James are eager and willing to do speaking engagements and training seminars of any kind. From keynotes to multi-day programs, the content will be customized, delivered to suit your organization's specific needs.

Ron James will share his experiences with anyone – from the classroom to the boardroom – and workshops can incorporate small-group activities, role-playing, case studies, video, statistics, and in-your-face questions. Presentation materials include tailored situational stories, participant guides, training materials and best-selling books.

To learn more about booking Kriss-Kross and Ron James for your next meeting, training or presentation:

Visit www.kriss-kross.org
Email jailtoday@aol.com
Call 1-855-JAIL2DAY

Also
Join Ron on Facebook: www.facebook.com/jailtoday

ronljames.com
ron@ronljames.com
717 433 2551

CPSIA information can be obtained at www.ICGtesting.com
Printed in the USA
BVOW05s1312010315

389703BV00005B/8/P